## DATE DUE

| | | | |
|---|---|---|---|
| | | | |
| | | | |
| | | | |
| | | | |
| | | | |
| | | | |
| | | | |
| | | | |
| | | | |
| | | | |
| | | | |
| | | | |
| | | | |
| | | | |
| | | | |
| | | | |
| | | | |

# EMI Control in the Design of Printed Circuit Boards

*with an optional floppy disk on EMI Problem-Solving Software*

**Donald R. J. White, MSEE/PE**



Publisher:
***The EEC Press***
**6193 Finchingfield Road**
**Gainesville, Virginia 22065 USA**
Phone: 540-347-0030 Fax: 540-347-5813

# EMI Control in the Design of Printed Circuit Boards

*with an optional floppy disk on EMI Problem-Solving Software*

**Volume 1**

*emf-emi control®, Inc.*
6193 Finchingfield Road
Gainesville, Virginia 22065 USA
Phone: 540-347-0030. Fax: 540-347-5813


**Published 1996**
**Printed in the United States of America**
**02 01 00 99 98 97 96 5 4 3 2 1**

**Library of Congress Card Number: 96-083828**
**ISBN: 0-932263-49-6**

# Acknowledgments

The author thanks his many seminar students, who have inspired this book set and Anna Byrne for her assistance in the production of this handbook.

# Other Handbooks Published by the EEC Press

### *The 12-Volume EMC Handbook Series*

(1) Duff, William G. - Vol. 1, *Fundamentals of EMC*, 1988
(2) Mardiguian, Michel - Vol. 2, *Grounding & Bonding*, 1988
(3) White, Donald R.J. and Mardiguian, Michael - Vol. 3, *Electromagnetic Shielding*, 1988
(4) White, Donald R.J. and Ecker, Jeffrey K. - Vol. 4, *Filter and Power Conditioning*, 1988
(5) Mardiguian, Michael - Vol. 5, *EMC in Components and Devices*, 1988
(6) Bronaugh, Edwin and Lambdin, William S. - Vol. 6, *EMI Test Methodology and Procedure*, 1994
(7) Duff, William G. - Vol. 7, *EMC in Telecommunications*, 1988
(8) Mardiguian, Michel - Vol. 8, *EMI Control Methodology and Procedures*, 1988
(9) Eckert, J.K. - Vol. 9, *Commercial EMC Standards of the USA*, 1988
(10) Wintzer, C. M. - Vol. 10, *International Commercial EMC Standards*, 1988
(11) Osburn, John D.M. - Vol. 11, *Military EMC Standards of USA*, 1988
(12) Osburn, John D.M. - Vol. 12, *Support Military Standards of USA*, 1988

### *The Six-Volume EMC Microwave Series*

(13) Georgopoulos, Chris, - Vol. 1, *Microwave Discrete Solid-State Devices & Interface Considerations*, 1990, 107 pages, 44 illustr.
(14) Georgopoulos, Chris, - Vol. 2, *Microwave Integrated Circuits & Interfaces*, 1990, 103 pages, 33 illustr.

(15) Georgopoulos, Chris, - Vol. 3, *RF and Microwave Matching Techniques*, 1990, 142 pages, 53 illustr.
(16) Georgopoulos, Chris, - Vol. 4, *Microwave Power Coupling & Related Interfacing Devices*, 1990, 12 pages, 44 illustr.
(17) Georgopoulos, Chris, - Vol. 5, *Driving Circuits & Interface for PIN Diode & Ferrite Phase Shifters*, 1990, 101 pages, 39 illustr.
(18) Georgopoulos, Chris, - Vol. 6, *Millimeter Waves & Applicable Interfaces*, 1990, 121 pages, 44 illustr.

### *Other EMC and EMF-Related Handbooks*

(19) Mardiguian, Michel, *Interference Control in Computer and Micro-Processor Based Equipment*, 1982
(20) Hart, William and Malone, Edgar - *Lightning and Lightning Protection*, 1988
(21) Gabrielson, Bruce, Dr., *The Aerospace Engineer's Handbook of Lightning Protection*, 1988
(22) Mardiguian, Michel, *How to Control Electrical Noise,* 1983
(23) Smith, Jr. Albert A, *Coupling of External Electromagnetic Fields to Transmission Lines*, 1989
(24) Mardiguian, Michel - *Electrostatic Discharge - Understand, Simulate and Fix ESD Problems* - 1994
(25) White, Donald R.J., *Electrical Filters - Synthesis, Design and Applications*, 1980
(26) Lewis, Warren, *Computer Site Integration Techniques,* 1993
(27) White, Donald; Barge, Mike; George, Eric; and Riley, Karl, *The EMF Controversy*, 1993
(28) White, Donald and Squires, Carl, *The EMF Cancer Scare,* 1994
(29) Denny, Hugh W., *Grounding for the Control of EMI,* 1983
(30) White, Donald R.J., *Shielding Design Methodology and Procedures* , 1986
(31) Georgopoulos, Chris, Dr., Fiber Optics & Optical Isolators, 1982
(32) Smith, Julius L., *Intermodulation Prediction and Control,* 1993
(33) White, Donald R.J., *EMI Control in the Design of Printed Circuit Boards*, 1996

Most of the above handbooks are also available on a CD-ROM. They may be purchased from *The EEC Press,* 6193 Finchingfield Road, Gainesville, Virginia 22065 USA. Phone: 540-347- 0030. Fax: 540-347-5813.

# Preface

This new handbook in our *Tech-Edge* series has been inspired by (1) developing new software on PCB radiation prediction and control and (2) presenting courses on *PCB Design for EMI Control*. I also wrote a handbook on the same subject, but it was 12 years ago. So much has changed in PCB EMI control that to update that book to a second edition would be more work than starting anew. Thus, I offer a brand new book in two volumes on the subject.

Perhaps the most fascinating aspect of these two volumes is the software which is sold as an option to the books. A floppy disk is located in a pocket on the inside back cover. The software allows users to predict radiated emission from PCBs and to compare this with any of a number of international EMI radiated RF regulations for compliance. If out-of-specifications, then the *"what-if mode"* can be used to exercise other variables, such as logic family; board layer trace height, trace width and length; number of IC-to-IC interconnect traces; average fanout; board dielectric constant; and top and/or bottom plane shield, if used.

## Volume 1

Chapter 1 presents introductory material to assist the non-EMC engineer to become familiar with the EMC vernacular. This also includes regulation and specification compliance. Chapter 2 gets right into the meat of PCB configurations. Issues of impedance control, single and 4-8 layer multilayer boards, phantom (image) ground planes, microstrip and stripline, ground-plane topics, logic families, and noise budgeting, are all addressed.

Chapter 3 shows how to predict logic radiation from PCB trace geometry and other design data. This allows determining quantitatively the level of radiation above or below specification. Since, usually out of specs, it also permits synthesizing the amount of overall shielding effectiveness needed for the outer box housing.

D-C power distribution and bussing comes first on the PCB, as discussed in Chap. 4. Decoupling capacitors, selection and their performance are also discussed. Then comes the clock circuits and data lines in Chap. 5. Guard traces, impedance control, vias, routing layers and trace termination criteria are all addressed.

## Volume 2

EMI-related, surface-mount components are presented in Chap. 6. These include capacitances, coils, filters and ferrites. Individual IC shields are also discussed. .

Crosstalk prediction and control is addressed in Chap. 7. More floppy-disk software, optionaly contained herein, is illustrated so that the reader can use the computer to do the crosstalk number crunching and "what-if" optimization gaming.

PCB layout, partitioning, fences, moats and bridges are discussed in Chap. 8.

Backplanes, motherboards and daughterboards are the subjects of Chap. 9. Extra shielding and impedance control are often needed here for radiation and noise budget compliance. Then, Chap. 10 discusses I/O connectors, cables and interconnects. Techniques for reducing common-mode current radiation from both the PCB and external cables are covered including the use of phantom-ground planes and segmented-ground planes.

Finally, Chap. 11 addresses diagnostic tools and measurements to help the designer accomplish the mission of reduced EMI radiation and susceptibility. EMSCAN offers an interesting composite diagnostic tool to locate where the radiating hot spots exist. Much less expensive, small magnetic-field probes, are also useful. Chap. 11 also dis- cusses EMI test chambers, GTEMPs, spectrum analyzers, and ESD generators.

I welcome any comments from the readers since the second edition of any book is in mind before the index of the first edition is complete. I also encourage a critique and ideas on the EMI problem-solving software.

Donald R.J. White
March 1996
Gainesville, Virginia USA

# Table of Contents

## EMI Control in the Design of Printed Circuit Boards

*Chapter 3 - Predicting PCB Radiation*



*Chapter 4 - Power Distribution and Bussing*



*Chapter 5 - Clock Circuits and Data Lines*



## Volume 2

*Chapter 6 - Surface Mounted Components*

# Chapter 1

# Some Basics of EMI-EMC

This chapter introduces the EMC vernacular so that non-EMC engineers and designers will understand the language. EMI regulations and specifications are addressed with the implications for EMI control. The prediction and analysis, radiation and crossstalk software, found in the pocket of the inside back cover if optionally ordered, is also discussed.

## 1.1 The EMI/EMC Vernacular

Every discipline has it own buzz words, alphabet soup and vernacular. EMC is no exception. So, here is the definition of about 25 terms that are frequently used in this handbook to assist the non EMC engineer.

Certification = Manufacturer sends its product and supporting information to the FCC for their checking to confirm that EMC compliance is met.
CE = Conducted Emission - current exiting from an electrical or electronic equipment along wires or cables which may or may not cause EMI.
CS = Conducted Susceptibility - current entering an electrical or electronic equipment along wires or cables which may or may not cause EMI.
dBμV/m = decibels above one microvolt per meter - a measure of electric-field strength.
dBμV = decibels above one microvolt - a measure of conducted emission or susceptibility.
DOC = Department of Communication - the regulatory agency tasked with EMI control requirements and enforcement in Canada.
EEC = European Economic Community - a consortium of 18 European countries acting as a regulatory body tasked with EMI control requirements and enforcement in Europe.
EMC = Electromagnetic Compatibility - the operating of electronic equipment and systems in their natural electromagnetic environment without disturbing other equipment and systems, and vice versa.
EMI = Electromagnetic Interference - the opposite of EMC in which an electronic equipment or system causes electromagnetic degradation of performance to one or more other equipments or systems.
ESD = Electrostatic Discharge = Triobelectric charging of a body (rubbing together of two insulators) which is then discharged into a conductor.
EU = European Union - a more recent term name for EEC.
EUT = Equipment under test.
$E^3$ = Electromagnetic Environmental Effects - includes all hostile eletromagnetic terms, including EMI, RFI, ESD, lightning and RADHAZ.
FCC = Federal Communications Commission - the regulatory agency tasked with EMI control requirements and enforcement in USA.
Ground Plane = a metal foil, sheet metal, or other flat-plane conductor acting as a return path to signal flow as well as EMI. It may not actually be grounded to an earthing conductor.
LISN = Line impedance Stabilization Network - a passive device placed between the power mains and its load to present a 50-ohm source impedance for testing purposes.

IEC = International Electrotechnical Commission - An organizational body tasked with coming up with limits, test methods and procedures for performing EMI measurements.
ITE = Information Technology Equipment - computing devices, computers, and their peripherals.
Microstrip = A trace and ground plane acting as a transmission line.
OEM = Original equipment manufacturer.
RADHAZ = Radiation hazards to equipment, ordnance, humans or fuels.
RE = Radiated Emission - electromagnetic radiation exiting from an electrical or electronic equipment which may or may not cause EMI.
RS = Radiated Susceptibility - electromagnetic radiation entering an electrical or electronic equipment which may or may not cause EMI.
RF Demodulation (Audio Rectification) - an EMI emission falling in the stopband of an analog or logic circuit, but causing it to undesirable respond.
RF = Radio Frequency = a frequency between 10 kHz and 300 GHz.
RFI = Radio-Frequency Interference = Similar to EMI, but excluding DC to 10 kHz, and in which at least one antenna is involved (the transmitter or receiver).
Stripline = A trace and two outboard ground planes acting as a transmission line.
Verification = Manufacturer performs his own tests to verify that his product complies with FCC rules and regulations. Sample of product is not sent to the FCC.

For more information, the reader should refer to the 115 EMC-related "engineering terms and definition" located in the floppy disk at the back of this handbook, if the disk has been optionally purchased. Therein is also located EMC tutorials and engineering tools.

## 1.2 EMC Regulations and Specifications

Allowable conducted and radiated EMI emission and immunity (susceptibility) are regulated by many nations. The military and certain other government agencies in USA use MIL-STD-461D levels of allowable EMI and MIL-STD-462 test methods and procedures.

The FCC regulates the non-government EMI emission from digital devices in USA under Part 15.B of the FCC Rules and Regulations. Requirements for connecting to the telephone network line comes under FCC R&R, Part 68.

European nations and some other countries require compliance with EU 336/89 EEC conducted and radiated emission and IEC 1000-4 family for conducted and radiated EMI immunity control.

## FCC Rules and Regulations, Parts 15.B EMI Emission Limits

For radiated emission compliance, measurements are made at a three-meter distance between the test item and the field-measuring antennas, deployed on a conduction plane meeting specific site attenuation requirements. The radiated limits for Class B compliance (for residential locations) are:

* 30 MHz to 88 MHz: 40 dBuV/m
* 88 MHz to 216 MHz: 43 dBuV/m
* Above 216 MHz: 46 dBuV/m

Class A (for industrial and commercial locations) allowable limits are 10 dB higher

## Exempted Devices

As long as they do not cause interference, the following equipment is exempted:

* Computing devices used aboard transportation vehicles, such as automobiles, aircraft and ships.

* Electronic systems used by public utilities or in industrial facilities.

* Digital devices used in industrial, commercial or medical test instruments.

* Digital devices used inside of electrical appliances such as washing machines, and dish washers.

* Special medical computing devices.

* Very low-power devices defined as those consuming less than 6 nW.

The FCC Bulletin No. 62 provides additional information on the exemptions.

## Subassemblies

The FCC recognizes that there is little benefit in regulating devices that are not sold to the end user such as plug-in cards and SMPS power supplies. Instead, they are incorporated into the finished product which must comply with Part 15.B. Some manufacturers, however, require their OEM suppliers to meet the regulations anyway since the switcher may incorporate its own filter and already be shielded (having low-level radiation from a 100 kHz switcher above 30 MHz).

If the *to-be-inserted PCB card* sold by the end user has a connector to permit connecting an external device via cables or wires (example PCMCIA cards), then the card must comply with the rules. But, if there is no external device connector and the product is not sold to the end user, the device does not have to comply.

## Labeling

With some exceptions, all Part 15 devices must show the following label:

This device complies with Part 15 of the FCC Rules. Operation is subject to the following two conditions:

(1) This device may not cause harmful interference, and

(2) This device must accept any interference received, including interference that may cause undesired operation.

Devices which are certified must also show their FCC identification number.

Users' manuals and related information must also warn of the possibility of interference.

## Test Reports

A test report is required whether certification or verification is used. Summaries of what must be included in a test report are given in FCC notices and ANSI standard C63.4. Additionally, the FCC has produced the "FCC Equipment Authorization Application Video," available from Telspan International by calling in USA, phone 301-731-5355.

Part 15 of the Federal Communications Commission Rules and Regulations addresses unlicensed electronic equipment. Devices are divided into three types:

(1) Intentional radiators are devices that intentionally generate and emit radio frequency by radiation or induction. Examples include garage-door openers and cordless telephones.

(2) Unintentional radiators are devices that intentionally generate radio-frequency energy for use within the device, or that send radio-frequency signals by conduction to associated equipment, but not intended to emit RF energy by radiation or induction. Examples include computers (using digital devices operating above 9 kHz), their peripherals and microprocessor-based equipment.

(3) Incidental radiators are devices that generate RF energy during the course of operation, but are not intentionally designed to do so. Examples include sparking at motor commutator-brushes, electromechanical relays and switches of inductive loads.

## Limits for Unintentional and Intentional Radiators

Section A of FCC, Part 15 discusses general requirements. Part B addresses the specifics of unintentional radiators, while Part C discusses the specifics of intentional radiators. The frequency range of each one is:

(1) Unintentional Radiators: from the lowest frequency generated in the device (but not below 9 kHz) up to the 10th harmonic of the highest frequency generated or 40 GHz, whichever is the lower.

(2) Intentional Radiators (for the highest internal frequency), the upper frequency to be measured is:

(a) Below 1.705 MHz internal, measure to 30 MHz.
(b) 1.705-108 MHz internal, measure up to 1 GHz.
(c) 105-500 MHz internal, measure up to 2 GHz.
(d) 500-1,000 MHz internal, measure up to 6 GHz.
(e) Above 1 GHz internal, measure up to the 5th harmonic of the highest internal frequency or 40 GHz, whichever is the lower.

Some manufactures design and test their products for Class A applications, even if exempted. This is perceived to give an edge on competition.

The FCC now allows manufactures to use the emission limits in CISPR 22 as an option to those in Part 15. If this option is selected, the device must still meet FCC requirements for radiation above 1 GHz, if applicable.

## Class A and B Devices

It has long been recognized that industrial facilities (if not exempted) and most commercial installations generate much more electrical noise than those in residential locations. As a result, the FCC has relaxed the conducted and radiation limits for commercially-located devices (Class A devices) by approximately 10 dB over residentially-located devices (Class B devices). If it is intended that any device serve both commercial and residential worlds, then it must comply with Class B limits, even though the intended use is primarily for commercial and industrial installations.

In order to get an edge on competition, many manufactures will design and test their equipments to comply with Class B limits, even though the intended use is for commercial and industrial installations.

## Conducted and Radiated Limits

Compliance for the test device must meet both conducted and radiated emission limits. For conducted, power-line emission is measured using an LISN (line impedance stabilization network) from 450 kHz to 30 MHz. The limits for Class B devices are 300 uV (50 dBuV) from 450 kHz to 1.6 MHz and 1000 uV (60 dBuV) from 1.6 MHz to 30 MHz. Class A limits are 10 dB higher.

## FCC Rules and Regulations, Part 68 - Connection to the Telephone Network

This subject is relevant to this book because many computers use modems to interface with the internet, world-wide web or otherwise to communicate through the telephone lines. As such, certain regulations must be followed to protect the telephone network.

There are five objectives in FCC establishing its Part 68, connecting to the telephone network:

*Checking for Hazardous Voltages and Current:* Hazardous voltages and current on telephone lines by customer equipment can damage central office equipment or injure personnel.

*Signal Power Limitations:* Signal levels must be maintained within maximum specified limits to prevent overloading and crosstalk.

*Maintaining Balance:* Line Balance must be maintained since imbalance causes increase in hum and crosstalk.

*On-Hook Impedance Limitations:* The central office uses specified impedances to evaluate condition of the lines and it must drive the telephone ringer.

*Billing Protection:* Certain delays and the absence of signals on prescribed signaling frequencies are required.

For information on Part 68 of the FCC Rules, contact: Richard Smith, at the FCC, 2000 M Street, NW suite 480, Washington, D.C. 20554. Phone: 202-418-2470

## EU 336/89 EEC - EMI Emission Limits

The European Economic Community (now called the European Union) issued EMC Directive 89/336 EEC, which specifies the following:

- Both conducted and radiated emission are regulated. EMI immunity is now of equal concern.
- Compliant equipment is labeled with the CE conformity mark.
- Manufacturers may choose either compliance to national or EU EMC regulations until 1 January 1996. Thereafter, EU EMC regulations apply.

With respect to the EMC directives:

▪ Unlike USA, a sovereign power, EU directives are binding on 15 nations, all members of the Common Market, which in turn are bound by Common Market treaties.

▪ This explains why EU directives are much slower in the making and approval process, and are more subject to change or modification.

▪ This is partly illustrated by postponing for three years the effective date of EU EMC directives until January 1, 1996.

▪ This is even more illustrated by the plethora of drafts, modifications, interpretations, cross referencing and confusion.

The table on the next page gives one index to the many EMC regulations and standards. It may not be complete or up to date at the time of this reading since it is perishable and changing.

| Test or Environment | Jan 1995 European Union Emissions and Immunity Standards for ITE Equipment | | |
|---|---|---|---|
| | Generic Industry Equip | Generic Light Industry | Information Tech. Eq. |
| Emission and Immunity Standards | EN50081-2/pr<br>EN50082-2(92) | EN50081-1<br>EN50082-1(92) | EN55022(87)<br>EN55024 (Draft) |
| HF Radiated Emissions<br>HF Conducted Emissions<br>LF Conducted Emissions<br><br>LF Flicker | EN55022 Class A<br>EN55022 Class A<br>EN60555-2<br>(82-1[92[ Annex)<br>EN60555-3<br>(82-1[ 92] Annex) | EN55022 Class B<br>EN55022 Class B<br>EN60555-2<br>(81-1 [92 ]Annex)<br>EN60555-3<br>(81-1[ 92] Annex) | EN55022 Class B & A<br>EN55022 Class B & A<br>EN61000-3-2<br>(except 96-97)<br>EN61000-3-3<br>(except 96-97) |
| Electrostatic Discharge (ESD) Immunity | (IEC 801-2 [1991])<br>4kV/8kV<br><br>Performance Criteria B | (IEC 801-2 [1984]<br>(use IEC 801-2 [1991])<br>4kV/8kV<br>Performance Criteria B | IEC-1000-4-4<br>4kV/8kV<br><br>Performance Criteria A |
| Radiated Electromagnetic Field Immunity | (IEC 801-3 [1984]<br>(use ENV50140)<br>3 V/m RMS 80% Mod,<br>1kHz<br>27-1000 MHz<br>27.1, 40.7, 433.9 MHz<br>10 V/m RMS | (IEC 801-3 [1984])<br>(use EN50140)<br>3 V/m RMS 80% Mod,<br>1 kHz<br>27-1000MHz<br><br>Performance Criteria A | ([Draft] IEC 1000-4-3)<br><br>3 V/m RMS 80% Mod,<br>1 kHz<br>80-1000 MHz<br>900 MHz 50% duty cycle<br>@200 Hz rate |
| Electrical Fast Transients (EFT) Immunity | (IEC 801-4 [1988])<br>2 kV CM (AC)<br>1 Kv CM (Sig)<br>Performance Criteria B | (IEC 804-4 [1988])<br>1 kV CM (AC)<br>0.5 Kv CM (Sig)<br>Performance Criteria B | (IEC 1000-4-4 DIS)<br>0.5 kV CM (AC)<br>0.5 kV CM (Sig)<br>Performance Criteria B |
| Electrical Power Line Surge Immunity | (IEC 1000-4-5 DIS)<br>prEN50082-2 Annex<br>2 kV CM, 1 kV DM (AC)<br>2 kV CM, 1 kV DM (Sig)<br><br>Performance Criteria B | (IEC 1000-4-5 DIS)<br>EN50082-1 Annex<br>2 kV CM, 1 kV DM (AC)<br>1 kV CM (Sig)<br><br>Performance Criteria B | (IEC 1000-4-4 DIS)<br>0.5 kV CM (AC)<br>12 Source<br>0.5 kV CM (Sig)<br>42 Source<br>Performance Criteria C |
| Injected RF Immunity | (IEC 1000-4-8)<br>prEN50082-2 Annex<br>3 V/150<br>0.15-80 MHz<br>80% Mod at 1 kHz<br>AC, Earth, Signal Ports<br>Performance Criteria A | (ENV50141)<br>EN50082-1 Annex<br>3 V/150<br>0.15-80 MHz<br>80% Mod at 1 kHz<br>AC, Signal Ports<br>Performance Criteria A | (IEC 1000-4-6 DIS)<br><br>3 V/150W 0.15-80 MHz<br>80% Mod at 1 kHz<br>AC, Signal Ports<br>Performance Criteria A |
| Magnetic Field Immunity | (IEC 1000-4-8)<br>prEN50082-2 Annex<br>30 A/m 50 Hz<br>Performance Criteria A | (IEC 1000-4-8)<br>EN50082-1 Annex<br>3 A/m 50 Hz<br>Performance Criteria A | (IEC 1000-4-88)<br><br>3 A/m 50 Hz<br>Performance Criteria A |
| Power Line Sag and Dropout Immunity | (IEC 1000-4-11 DIS)<br>prEN50082-2 Annex<br>30% 0.5 cy B<br>60% 5.0 cy C<br>>95% 5.0 Sec C<br>Performance as above | (prEN50093)<br>EN50082-1 Annex<br>30% 0.5 cy B<br>50% 5.0 cy C<br>.95% 5.0 Sec C<br>Performance as above | (IEC 1000-4-11 DIS)<br><br>.95% 250 cy C<br>30% 25 cy B<br>.95% 1/2 cy B<br>Performance as above |

Performance Level:
A - No change in operation, no loss of data
B - Temporary change in operation, automatic recovery, no loss of data
C - No damage, manual intervention OK

Prefix/Suffix Explanations:
pr - Pre-release
DIS - Final Version, except editorial changes only
ENV - Pre-Standard to be used until release of final standard
Annex- Test proposed for inclusion in Generic after standard is released

Courtesy of Bill Ritenour, Segate Technology

## IEC 1000-4 Immunity Requirements

The IEC 801 (International Electrotechnical Commission) series of standards provide the basic international standards for immunity of electronic products. The IEC 801 series cover immunity of electronic products to ESD, RF fields, electrically fast transients, surges and several other phenomena. Recently, the nomenclature of the 801 series was changed to the 1000-4 series. For example, IEC 801-2, which covers specific immunity to ESD is now called IEC 1000-4-2. The final dash number (in this case 2) in the 1000-4 series is consistent with the final dash number in the 801 series.

## IEC-1000-4-2 (IEC 801-2) Electrostatic Discharge

The 1991 edition of IEC 801-2 specifies two modes of operation for an ESD-simulated generator: an air discharge mode and a direct-contact discharge mode. In the air-discharge mode, a spark from the test probe of the ESD generator is discharged into the air toward the equipment under test (EUT). The generator must be able to provide an adjustable charging voltage up to 15 kV. The discharge level, which the EUT must withstand, depends on its type and the environment in which it is intended to be used.

In the direct-contact discharge mode, an impulse is released from the ESD generator. The tip of the generator's probe is in actual contact with the EUT when the discharge is released. For this mode, the generator should be able to provide an adjustable voltage up to 8 kV, and the rise time for the direct-contact pulse must be between 0.7-1.0 nanoseconds.

### IEC 1000-4-3 (IEC 801-3) RF Electromagnetic Fields

IEC 801-3 is concerned with the immunity of electronic equipment when subjected to radiated electromagnetic fields, such as those generated by radio transceivers or any other device that will generate continuous-wave, radiated electromagnetic energy. IEC 801-3 establishes a test procedure and test levels that can be used as a common reference against which to test equipment. The testing frequency range is between 27 MHz and 600 MHz. The severity of the RF fields varies from 1 to 10 volts/m depending on the type of equipment and the operating RF environment.

### IEC 1000-4-4 (IEC 801-4) RF Electrical Fast Transients

Electrical-fast transients (EFT) occur as a result of arcing contacts in switches and relays. EFT disturbances are common in industrial environments

IEC 801-4 specifies the EFT threat in both power and data lines.

In the current revision of IEC 801-4, the output occurs as a burst of high voltage spikes at a repetition rate of 5 kHz for peak voltages less than 1 kV and 2.5 kHz for a peak voltage of 2 kV. (IEC 1000-4-4) will raise the maximum transient frequency repetition rate to 100 kHz at all voltage levels.) The burst length is defined as 15 ms (1ms for the 100 kHz test in IEC-1000-4-4) with bursts repeated every 300 ms. The burst sequence is to last over a time interval to be specified at no less than 1 minute. Each individual burst pulse has a rise time of 5 ns with a total duration of 50 ns.

The open circuit voltage threat level varies from 0.5 kV to 4kV for power lines and from 0.25 kV to 2 kV for data lines. The threat level that applies depends on the type of equipment and the operating environment.

## 1.3 Basic Elements of EMI

It takes both a source and victim to produce EMI. Examples of each are shown in Fig. 1.1. Often more difficult to identify and define is the coupling path between

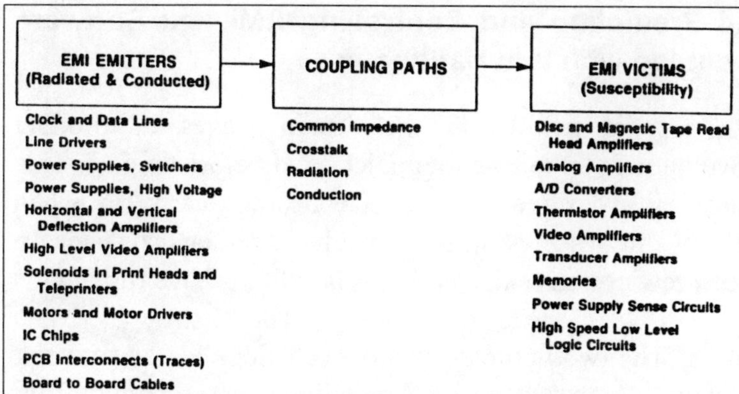

Fig. 1.1 - Basic elements of an emission-susceptibility situation

source and victim. Several such paths are also shown in the central listing in Fig. 1.1.

When the EMI source is an intentional transmitter, it will also radiate harmonics, albeit at much lower levels than the fundamental. When the source is a PCB, clock and data-line harmonics are also generated, but fall off less rapidly than an intentional transmitter. In either case, the harmonics can appear in the passband of intentional receivers and cause EMI.

In some respects, if not controlled, the PCB example can be more damaging as a source, since its fundamental radiations may also appear in the passband of an intentional receiver. On the other hand, the intentional fundamental from a transmitter, often being orders of magnitude higher than that from PCBs, can cause R-F demodulation (audio rectification) in most electronic victims if not protected.

## 1.4 Predicting and Controlling EMI and Software included with this Handbook.

It is helpful in the design stages of product development to be able to predict EMI before the fact. This allows the designer to optimize designs early on when several options may still be available rather than later on when few options exist, and time and funds have run out.

The two volumes of this Tech-Edge PCB handbook explain how to control EMI radiations and crosstalk. But, the optional software makes things come alive. Fast prediction, analysis and fix are now available to permit optimization, not possible when done by manual methods.

Chapter 3 is especially offered for focusing in on predicting radiation from traces and PCBs. It gives the math models so that the user will know where the emphasis needs to go. It also provides software (if separately purchased) for accomplishing this very rapidly vs. the tedious manual prediction and number-crunching process.

Chapter 7 focuses in on crosstalk prediction and control. It also gives the math models so that the user will know which variables to manipulate. Software is provided (if purchased separately) for quickly achieving this.

Other EMI problem-solving software, included in the floppy disk are:

- Predicting and Controlling Common-Mode Current Radiation from PCB I/O Cables.
- Shielding effectiveness of Equipment Metalized Housing.
- Shield Aperture Leakage Prediction and Control.
- Several other EMC Tools to facilitate computation

## 1.5 How to use this Handbook

The principal purpose of this handbook is (1) to transfer information and techniques to permit designing PCBs that will comply with one or more national EMC regulations and standards and (2) to limit self jamming from crosstalk and other internal EMI and from external EMC radiations. Most of the chapters provide material to assist in accomplishing this. This book is not intended to address how to design logic networks and PCBs to support them.

The index is considerably more comprehensive than normal. This should help the reader find what he seeks.

## 1.6 References:

Boxleitner, W., "Electrostatic Discharge and Electronic Equipment," *IEEE Press*, 1988.

Dockey, R.W. and German, R.F., New Techniques for Reducing Printed Circuit Board Common-Mode Radiation," *IEEE Inter- national EMC Symposium,* Dallas, Texas, August 9-13, 1993, pp. 334-339.

Drewniak, J.L.; Hubing, T.H. and Van Doren, T.P, Investigation of Fundamental Mechanisms of Common-Mode Radiation from PCB with Attached Cables, *IEEE International Symposium on Electromagnetic Compatibility,* 1994, pp. 110-115.

German, R.F.; Ott, H.; and Paul, C.R., "Effect of an Image Plane on Printed Circuit Board Radiation," *IEEE International Symposium on Electromagnetic Compatibility,* Wash. D.C., August 21-23, 1990, pp. 284-291.

Gerke, D. and Kimmel, W., "The Designers' Guide to Electromagnetic Compatibility," *EDN*, Jan. 20, 1994.

Heinke, R., "EMC Controlled PCB Design," Conference Record of the EMC EXPO, *Interference Control Technologies, Inc.,* 1989.

Hill, R.L.; Van Doren, T.; Hubling, T.; and Drewniak, Y., "Common-Mode Currents Induced on Wires Attached to Multi-Layer, Printed-Wire Boards with Segmented Ground Planes," *IEEE International Symposium on Electromagnetic Compatibility*, Chicago, Illinois, August 22-26, 1994, pp. 116-120.

Hsu, T, "The Validity of Using Image-Plane Theory to Predict PCB Radiation," *IEEE International Symposium on Electromagnetic Compatibility,* 1991, pp. 58-60

Mardiguian, M., "Controlling Radiated Emissions by Design," *Van Nostrand Reinhold*, 1992.

Montrose, M.I., "Overview of Design Techniques for Printed Circuit Board Layout Used in High-Technology Products," *IEEE International Symposium on Electromagnetic Compatibility,* 1991

Montrose, M.I., "Printed Circuit Board Design Techniques for EMC Compliance," *IEEE Press,* 1995

Motorola, "Semiconductor Master Selection Guide," 03/95, Revision 8, Motorola, Inc.

Ott, H., "Noise Reduction Techniques in Electronic Systems," *John Wiley & Sons,* 1988

Parker, C.U., "Choosing a Ferrite for the Suppression of EMI," *Fair-Rite Products, Inc.*, 1988.

Paul, C.R., "Effectiveness of Multiple Decoupling Capacitors," *IEEE Transactions on Electromagnetic Compatibility*, EMC-34, pp. 130-133.

Paul, C.R. and Bush, D., "Radiated EMI from Common-Mode Currents," *IEEE International Symposium on Electromagnetic Compatibility*, Atlanta, 1987.

Ritenaur, Bill, "European EMC Regulations for Information Technology Equipments," *MC Test and Design,* November-December 1994.

White, Donald R.J. , "EMI Controlling the Design of Printed Circuit Boards and Backplanes," *Don White Consultants, Inc.,* 1982.

# Chapter 2

# Printed Circuit Board Fundamentals

Impedance control and the microstrip and stripline trace transmission-line media are covered. Single through eight-layer boards are discussed together with segmented and phantom ground planes for radiation emission reduction. Logic families are analyzed with respect to relative noisiness and immunity control.

## 2.1 Impedance Control

At low frequencies, where the length of an interconnecting trace between a driving gate and driven gate is a tiny fraction of a wavelength ($\lambda$), it doesn't matter what the characteristic impedance ($Z_o$) is of the trace. The trace load is seen directly by the source. So, $Z_o$ can have any value and can vary over its length with no performance impact.

When the length of the interconnecting trace approaches about $0.05\lambda$, the trace length begins to impact the load as seen at the driving end. $Z_o$ begins to have its impact for the same reason. If $Z_o$ is not well behaved (does not vary) over its length, the performance starts to become unpredictable and uncertain. Thus, control of characteristic impedance for high-speed logic (risetime $<5$ nsec) requires that the transmission line be well defined and stabilized over its entire length ($0.05\lambda_{\text{dielectric}} = 13$ cm for PCBs with dielectric constants of about 4). Contrast this with older double-sided, single layer boards, whose logic families had/have risetimes of 50 nsec. Here, the entire dimension of the board $\ll 0.05\lambda$. So, impedance control is unnecessary.

When the trace length $> 0.05\lambda$, poor impedance match and/or abrupt changes in trace impedance cause VSWRs (voltage standing wave ratios) significantly greater than 1. This leads to pulse distortion, back-porching, overshoot/undershoot and ringing, and corresponding consumption of the noise budget allocated from the noise-immunity level. This, in turn, increases the bit-error rate or otherwise compromises overall performance.

## 2.2 Microstrip and Stripline Transmission Lines

Table 2.1 shows three transmission lines using traces etched on printed-circuit boards. The first and the third are used mostly on double-sided, single layer boards, where good impedance control is generally not necessary.

Table 2.1 - Characteristic impedance of conductor pairs

| | 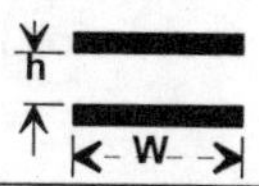 | 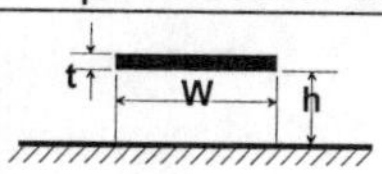 | 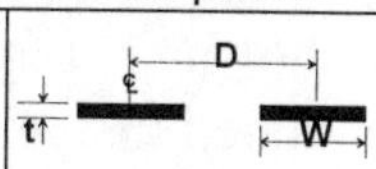 |
|---|---|---|---|
| **W/h or D/W** | **$Z_{01}$ = Parallel Strips** | **$Z_{02}$ = Strip Over Ground Plane** | **$Z_{03}$ = Strips Side-by-Side** |
| 0.5 | 377 | 377 | NA |
| 0.6 | 281 | 281 | NA |
| 0.7 | 241 | 241 | N/A |
| 0.8 | 211 | 211 | NA |
| 0.9 | 187 | 187 | NA |
| 1.0 | 169 | 169 | 0 |
| 1.1 | 153 | 153 | 25 |
| 1.2 | 140 | 140 | 34 |
| 1.5 | 112 | 112 | 53 |
| 1.7 | 99 | 99 | 62 |
| 2.0 | 84 | 84 | 73 |
| 2.5 | 67 | 67 | 87 |
| 3.5 | 48 | 48 | 107 |
| 4.0 | 42 | 42 | 114 |
| 5.0 | 34 | 34 | 127 |
| 6.0 | 28 | 28 | 137 |
| 7.0 | 24 | 24 | 146 |
| 8.0 | 21 | 21 | 153 |
| 9.0 | 19 | 19 | 160 |
| 10.0 | 17 | 17 | 166 |

Note: Mylar dielectric assumed, $\varepsilon_r = 5.0$

Paper-base phenolic or glass epoxy assumed; $\varepsilon_r = 4.7$

$Z_{01} = (377/\sqrt{\varepsilon_r})h/W$, for W> 3h and h>3t

$Z_{02} = (377/\sqrt{\varepsilon_r})h/W$, for W> 3h

$Z_{03} = (120/\sqrt{\varepsilon_r})\ln_e[D/W + \sqrt{(D/W)^2-1}]$, for W>>t

The best impedance control is achieved by using microstrip and strip transmission lines. Actually, microstrip is not quite as good as stripline since some of the fringing field exists above the outside-layer dielectric as shown in Fig. 2.1. When this is the component side, a device may be positioned above the microstrip trace which would alter its characteristic impedance. This cannot happen for stripline, as shown in Fig. 2.2, where all the field configuration is contained inside as in a coaxial line.

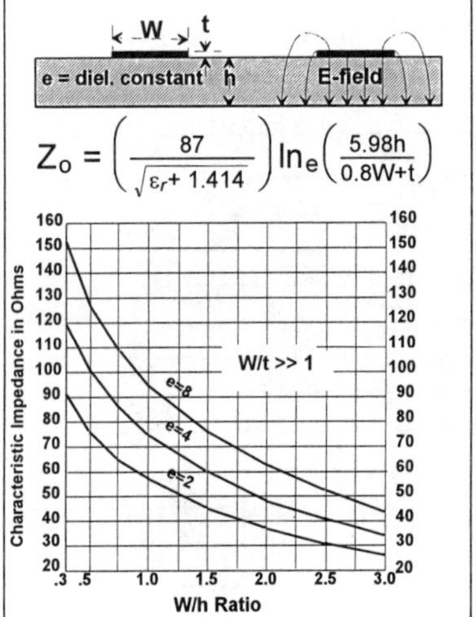


Fig. 2.1 - Microstrip transmission lin

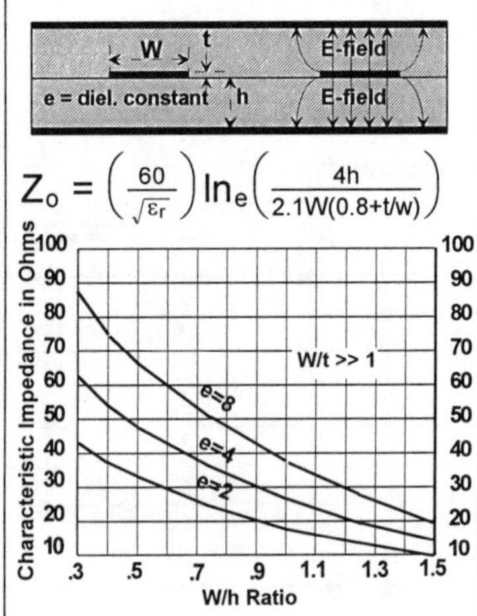


Fig. 2.2 - Stripline transmission line

Microstrip, used on the component and solder sides of a multilayer board, of course, radiates to the outside world. Except at the board edge, stripline cannot radiate since its use is relegated exclusively to internal layers. Thus, to control microstrip radiation, one approach is to use a shield layer on both outsides of a multilayer board. The military often does this, especially where items are expendable, whereas industrial applications do not in order to reduce cost and permit board repair.

The equations for the characteristic impedance of microstrip and stripline are both shown in Figs. 2.1 and 2.2. The graphic plots are valid for W/t>>1. Note that stripline tends to have a characteristic impedance much less than microstrip. The reason is similar to why coaxial lines have a lower impedance than balanced two-wire lines. In using either line, employ the *3-W rule*, in which the trace is located:

(1) near the edge of a PCB by not closer than a distance of three times the trace width to keep board edge radiation below 60 dB.

(2) next to another signal or clock trace by not less than three times the trace width to maintain crosstalk below some unspecified level. However, as described later, clock traces are usually protected by guard traces. Actual trace separation and crosstalk are discussed in Chap. 7.

## 2.3 PCB Materials and Propagation Velocity

The velocity, $V_a$, of light and RF energy in air is:

$$V_a = 3 \times 10^8 \text{ meters/sec} = 30 \text{ cm/nsec} \qquad (2.1)$$

The velocity, $V_\varepsilon$, of RF propagation in any media, having a relative dielectric constant, $\varepsilon_r$, is:

$$V_\varepsilon = 3 \times 10^8/\sqrt{\varepsilon_r} \text{ m/s} = 30/\sqrt{\varepsilon_r} \text{ cm/nsec} \qquad (2.2)$$

PCB materials are available for PCBs having relative dielectric constants from 2 to 15. Some are listed in Tab. 2.2. The higher dielectric constant boards have the advantage of permitting compressing the real estate of each dimension by the square root of the dielectric material. This also tends to increase the capacitance and decrease the characteristic impedance of the microstrip or stripline.

Table 2.2 - Some PCB dielectric materials

| Dielectric Constant | Dielectric Material | Source |
|---|---|---|
| 2.1-2.45 | Woven Glass/Teflon | GPY/GY |
| 2.2 | Teflon | GPY/GC |
| 2.2-2.4 | Nonwoven Glass/Teflon | FR-5/GP |
| 2.2-2.4 | Nonwoven Glass/Teflon | FR-5/GR |
| 2.4-2.6 | Woven Glass/Teflon | FR-5/GX |
| 2.6-2.8 | Woven Glass/Teflon | FR-5/GT |
| 3.0-3.8 | Woven Quartz/Polyimide | GPY/QI |
| 3.5 | Polyimide | GPY/GC |
| 3.6-4.4 | Woven Aramid/Polyimide | GPY/AI |
| 3.8-4.5 | Woven Aramid/Epozy | GPY/AE |
| 4.0-4.7 | Woven Glass/Polyimide | GPY/GI |
| 4.0-4.7 | Woven Glass/BT | GPY/GM |
| 4.0-4.7 | Woven Glass/Cyanate Ester | GPY/GC |
| 4.2-4.9 | Woven Glass/Epoxy | FR-4/GF |
| 4.2-4.9 | Woven Glass/Epoxy | FR-5/GH |
| 4.2-4.9 | Nonwoven Polyester/Epoxy | GPY/CF |

## 2.4 Double-Sided, Single-Layer Boards

As mentioned earlier, double-sided, single-layer boards are still in use today. Their earlier use is based on simplicity of layout and speed to get the design back from the layout or CAD draftsmen. They are intended for low or medium-speed (risetime > 10 nsec) logic families having DIP (dual in-line) package configurations. Three layouts are shown in Figs. 2.3-2.5, ranging from bad practices to best.

Figure 2.3 is a bad layout since the self inductance of the traces dominates rather than mutual inductances which reduce overall trace inductance. No trace flux linkage makes the path impedance much higher, since $L_{overall} = L_{self} - L_{mutual}$ and $Z_0 = \sqrt{L/C}$ . The loop areas are also excessive making trace radiation and crosstalk very high.

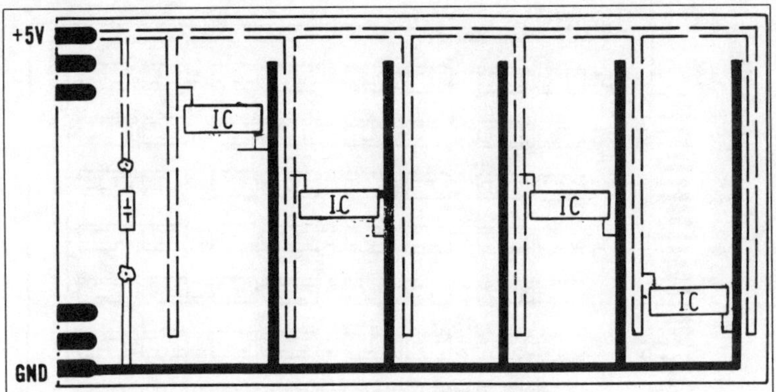


Fig. 2.3 - Bad PCB power distribution layout

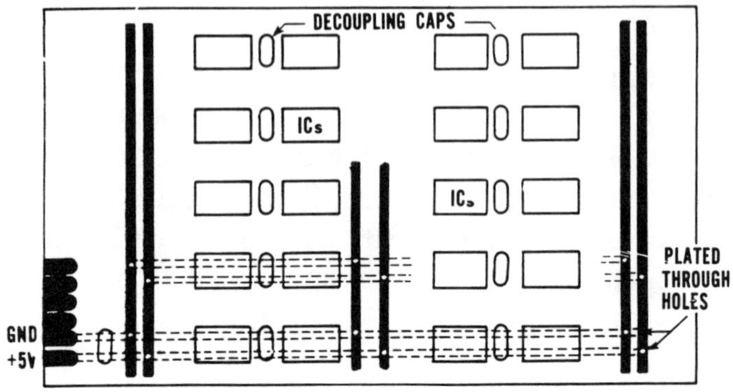


Fig. 2.4 - Better power distribution vs. Fig. 2.3

Figure 2.4 is a much better layout reducing power distribution impedance and signal trace areas. The corresponding radiation and crosstalk reduction result. Figure 2.5 is a further extension of Fig. 2.4 into a matrix for best power distribution for double-sided, single-layer boards.

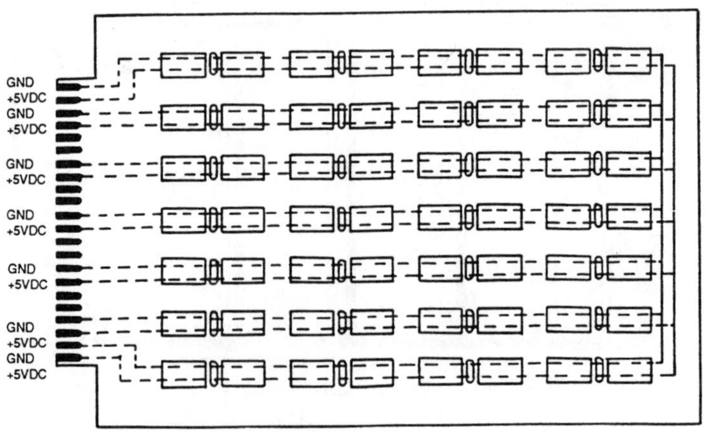


Fig. 2.5 - Best power-distribution layout.

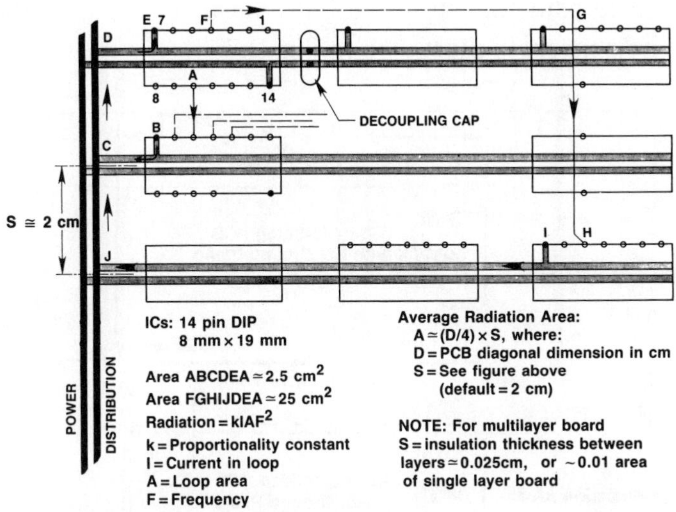


Fig. 2.6 - Inter IC chip communication.

The problem with double-sided, single-layer boards is the path that the signal current takes in getting from a driving gate in one IC to a driven gate in another IC. This is illustrated in Fig. 2.6, where large loop areas result in excessive radiation and crosstalk.

## 2.5 Phantom or Image Ground Plane

The large loop area in Fig. 2.6 is defined by path FGHIJDEF. How is this loop area to be reduced? One approach for single and double-layer boards is to add a ground plane, very close to the top and/or bottom traces (the closer the better). This induces (via magnetic coupling) an image of the trace which provides a much lower impedance path for return current than that shown in Fig. 2.6. The concept is illustrated in Fig. 2.7.

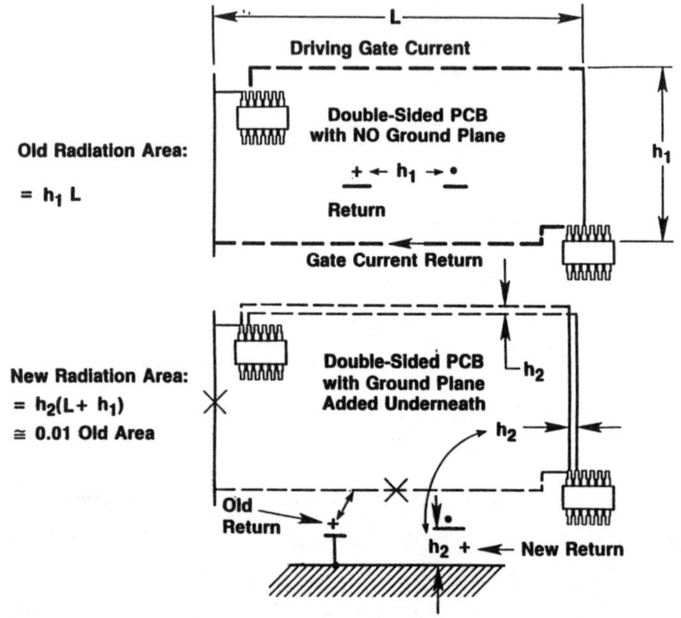


Fig. 2.7 - Reducing radiation from a single-layer PCB by adding an image-ground plane.

Return current will then follow both that of Fig. 2.6 and the phantom image-ground plane (Fig. 2.7) in parallel. The image plane is a usually a single 1-ounce copper foil (foil thickness = 1.4 mils = 36 um) PCB, placed directly against the solder side with the foil on the outside. Alternatively, coat the foil with insulation and place it against the solder tabs, ensuring that the insulation is protected. The phantom ground plane in Fig. 2.7 will reduce radiation from the double-sided, single-layer board by 20-30 dB over that of Fig. 2.6.

## 2.6 Multi-Layer Boards

The purpose of multi-layer boards is to overcome the problems of the double-sided, single-layer board. These are:

- Poor impedance control
- Large chip interconnect loop areas

Resulting in:

- Poor pulse waveshape
- Excessive radiation
- Excessive crosstalk

Multi-layer boards also permit greater circuit packing density and/or reduce PCB real estate.

### Four-Layer Boards

Figure 2.8 is the most popular and simplist of multi-layer boards. Signal-1 trace on Layer-1 forms a microstrip with the ground plane on Layer-2. Similarly, Signal-2 trace on Layer-4 (usually the solder side) forms an inverted microstrip line with the power plane on Layer-3. While Layers-1 and -2 make a sound microstrip, Layers-3 and -4 do not, as explained below.

The low characteristic impedance (typically of the order of 100 mohms) of power-ground planes is good for power distribution. But, both planes contain all manner of noise due to sudden current surges from toggling logic gates. Many logic devices exhibit asymmetrical pull-up/ pull-down currents. This results in better magnetic-flux cancellations (induced trace image return) in the ground plane with its mating signal trace, than a trace using a power plane for its return. The net effect is to cause greater circuit-path inductance in the power plane which causes enhanced radiation and crosstalk for traces imaging on the power plane.

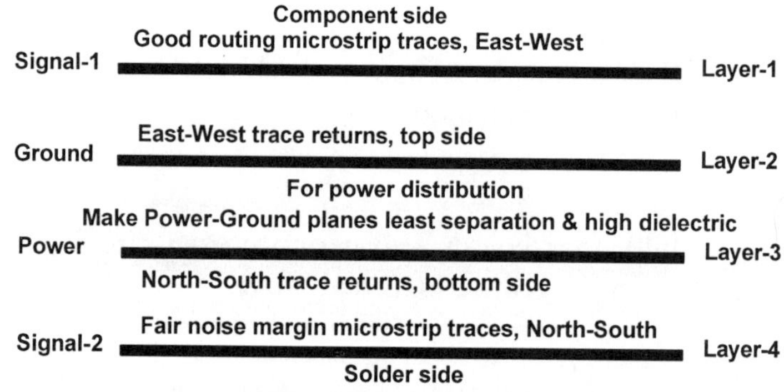


Fig. 2.8 - Popular four-layer board

For the above reason, Signal-2 on Layer-4 in Fig. 2.8 does not perform as well (is noiser due to less flux cancellation) as Signal-1 on Layer-1.

## Six-Layer Boards

More options for signal trace routing and reducing PCB radiation are offered in six-layer boards. But, depending upon the selected configurations, some perform better than others with respect to overall PCB radiation.

Figure 2.9 is a fair-performing arrangement vs. other

options. The problem is that two outer-stacked signal trace layers (Layer-1 and Layer-2) appear above a single ground plane (Layer-3). This increases radiation by about twice (6 dB) compared to a single-trace layer above a ground plane due to the double layer height of Signal-1. A similar situation exists for Layers 4-6. Additionally, the bottom trace Layers-5 and -6 are returning their image currrent on the power plane, which does not cancel flux linkages as well, as described above for four-layer boards.

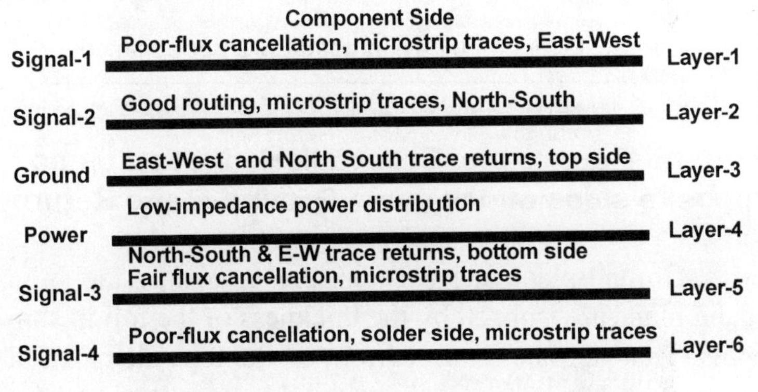


Fig. 2.9 - Six-layer board having fair EMC performance

The six-layer board configuration shown in Fig. 2.10 resolves the EMI-control problem shown in Fig. 2.9. In Fig. 2.10, all signal-trace currents are returned through an adjacent ground-plane to permit good flux coupling. A filler layer is used to force Signal-2 to couple to ground Layer-2 much more than to the power plane. The penalty is an extra ground-plane layer at the loss of a signal layer.

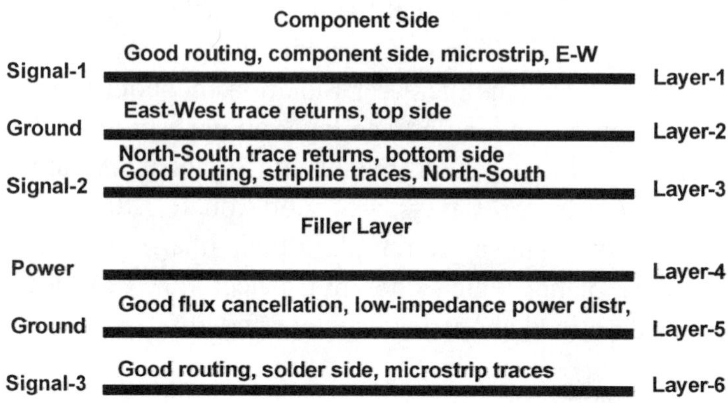


Fig. 2.10 - Six-layer board having good EMC performance

## Ground Bounce and Crosstalk Reduction using Opposite sides of the same Ground-Plane Return

Ground-plane currents on the opposite side of a ground plane are isolated by the thickness of the foil in skin depths. Thus, a trace-return current on the top side of a foil does not common-impedance couple to a trace-return current on the bottom of a foil as shown in Layer-2 in Fig. 2.10. This then means less crosstalk and ground bounce. To demonstrate this:

The skin depth of a copper-foil return, ground-image plane is:

$$0.066/\sqrt{f_{MHz}} \quad \text{mm} \qquad (2.3)$$

$$2.6/\sqrt{f_{MHz}} \quad \text{mils} \qquad (2.4)$$

where, $f_{MHz}$ = frequency in MHz

For example, for a one-ounce copper-foil (thickness = 1.4 mils or 36 um) ground plane at 100 MHz, a skin depth is 0.26 mils. Thus, the foil corresponds to 1.4/0.26 = 5.4 skin depths. So, surface currents on opposite sides of a one-ounce foil are decoupled by 5.4 skin depths or attenuated by 8.69 dB/skin depth = 47 dB.

When 1/2-oz foils are used (e.g., PCMCIA cards), the benefit is reduced since decoupling is then 23 dB. Thus, common-impedance coupling begins to occur, resulting in increased ground bounce and crosstalk.

## Eight-Layer Boards

The eight-layer PCB is a continuation of the layout concepts discussed above. There are both poor and good configurations relative to impedance control and EMI radiation.

Figure 2.11 illustrates a typical layout by many board designers who may not be aware of poorer impedance, radiation and crosstalk control than provided by other options. The double-stacked signal Layers-1 and -2 and Layers-7 and -8 are both on the outside of the PCB layout (component and solder sides). Thus, radiation is the greatest. Also, the impedance of the two outer layers is greater than the impedance of the two layers next to the ground and power planes (Layers-4 and -5). Thus, impedance matching to the driven gates will differ and greater signal reflections will result in consuming more noise budget of the available logic noise-immunity level. Poorer (weaker) signal-image plane returns in the power plane result in greater returns coupled to other paths (e.g., the signal plane) with resulting poorer impedance control and increased crosstalk and radiation.

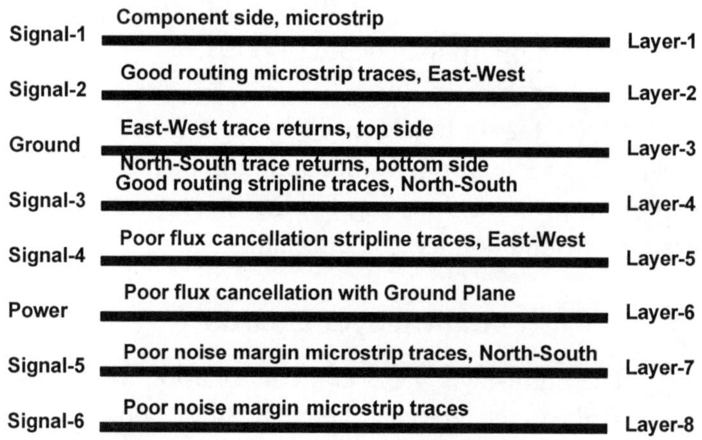


Fig. 2.11 - Eight-layer board having poor EMI control

EMI problems in the above eight-layer board are eliminated in the arrangement shown in Fig. 2.12. Therein, every signal layer is faced against a ground, image-plane return to permit good impedance match and crosstalk control. Only the two outside layers will radiate and at lower levels because of lower loop areas (one layer height only to a ground plane) compared to the layout of Fig. 2.11. The penaltly for the use of Fig. 2.12 is two more ground-plane layers (or two less signal layers). When the PCB designer is relatively unknowledgeable of EMI control, he will naturally opt for Fig. 2.11 vs. Fig. 2.12.

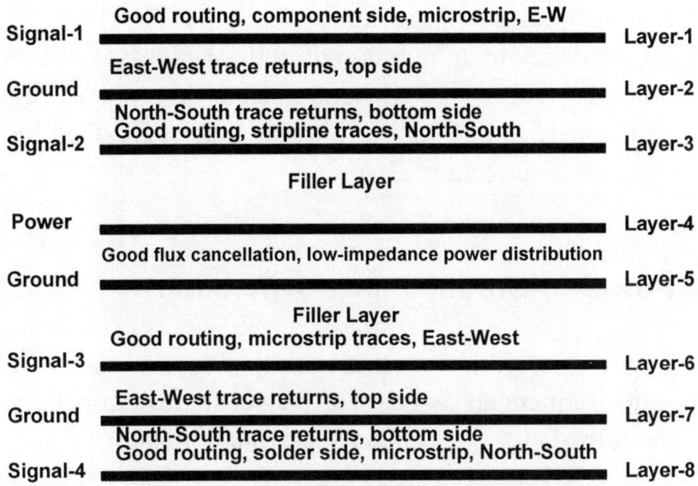


Fig. 2.12 - Eight-layer board having good EMI control

## 2.7 Signal-to-Ground Plane Separation

As discussed in the last section, the EMC mission is:

- reduce radiation via smaller driving-gate-to-driven-gate, trace-loop areas. This means lower trace height above its image-return plane.
- reduce crosstalk which is also proportional to smaller driving-gate-to-driven-gate, trace-loop areas. This also means lower trace height above its image-return plane.

Each EMI-control measure involves lower trace height. As shown in Figs. 2.1 and 2.2, this means lower transmission-line characteristic impedance for both microstrip and stripline. This may not always be an advantage depending upon the logic family used (see Section 2.11) when impedance matching is required for high-speed logic. This occurs when the driving-gate-to-driven-gate trace length exceeds about $15/\sqrt{\varepsilon_r}$ cm per nanosecond of logic rise- time as discussed in Chap. 5.

## 2.8 Power-to-Ground Plane Separation

Obviously, lower source impedance at clock and data-rate frequencies is best for power distribution (Chap. 4). The impedance, $Z_o$, of a power-ground plane is:

$$Z_o = \frac{120\pi h}{d\sqrt{\varepsilon_r}} \tag{2.5}$$

where, h = layer separation or inside distance between power and ground planes.

d = smaller dimension of the two-dimension parallel plane.

$\varepsilon_r$ = relative dielectric constant of the substrate layer relative to air.

For convenience, Eq. (2.5) is tabulated in Tab. 2.3 for several values of h/d ratios and dielectric constants. Many boards today have an h/d of about .001 and dielectric constant of about 4. Thus, their delivery power planes have source impedances of about 380 mohms. As the two mil materials (using 1/2-oz. copper foil) become more widely used in PCMCIA-card applications, source impedances of about 90 mohms become achievable. Consequently, inter-gate switching currents of 20 mA will result in voltage

Table 2.3 - Characteristic impedance in mohms of power-ground plane power distribution

| Dielectric Constant | h/d Ratios of Parallel Plane | | | | | | | | | |
|---|---|---|---|---|---|---|---|---|---|---|
| | **.0003** | **.0005** | **.0007** | **.001** | **.002** | **.003** | **.005** | **.007** | **.01** | **.02** |
| 2 | 80 | 134 | 186 | 267 | 534 | 800 | 1,340 | 1,860 | 2,670 | 5,340 |
| 2.5 | 72 | 120 | 168 | 240 | 480 | 720 | 1,200 | 1,680 | 2,400 | 4,800 |
| 3 | 65 | 109 | 151 | 217 | 433 | 650 | 1,090 | 1,510 | 2,170 | 4,330 |
| 3.5. | 60 | 100 | 140 | 200 | 400 | 600 | 1,000 | 1,400 | 2,000 | 4,000 |
| 4 | 57 | 95 | 133 | 190 | 380 | 570 | 950 | 1,330 | 1,900 | 3,800 |
| 4.5 | 53 | 89 | 123 | 177 | 353 | 530 | 890 | 1,230 | 1,770 | 3,530 |
| 5 | 51 | 85 | 119 | 170 | 340 | 510 | 850 | 1,190 | 1,700 | 3,400 |
| 6 | 46 | 77 | 108 | 154 | 307 | 462 | 770 | 1,080 | 1,540 | 3,070 |
| 7 | 43 | 72 | 100 | 143 | 287 | 430 | 720 | 1,000 | 1,430 | 2,870 |
| 10 | 36 | 60 | 84 | 120 | 240 | 360 | 600 | 840 | 1,200 | 2,400 |
| 12 | 33 | 54 | 76 | 109 | 217 | 326 | 540 | 760 | 1,090 | 2,170 |
| 15 | 29 | 49 | 68 | 97 | 193 | 290 | 490 | 680 | 970 | 1,930 |

drops (ground bounce) of less than 2 mV to protect the new 3 Volt $V_{cc}$, lower noise-immunity level logic.

## 2.9 Segmented Ground Planes and Reducing PCB Common-Mode Radiation

A multi-layer board with a good ground plane can produce common-mode radiation similar to a dipole antenna. This ground plane is commonly thought of as a low-impedance path for returning trace currents and one which is of constant potential across its area. In fact, these currents give rise to voltage gradients in the plane which act as sources of common-mode current.

The majority of the R-F current flowing along a signal trace on a multi-layer PCB returns on the ground plane directly beneath the signal trace. However, a small portion of the ground-plane current also can return via indirect paths causing the PCB and attached cables, if present, to produce common-mode radiation similar to a dipole antenna. These emissions may be reduced by decreasing the distance between the signal trace and the ground plane, by providing additional low-impedance paths for the signal current, and by placing an image plane above the PCB and connecting it to the ground plane around its periphery.

Segmented ground planes in multi-layer boards are also useful in reducing common-mode radiation from cables. Effective gap lengths of about 2-3 cm., perpendicular to the dominant ground plane current flow, produces reduced common-mode radiations. Significant quantitative data on the effectiveness of this technique is not available at the time of this writing. This is discussed further in Volume 2.

## 2.10 The Power-Ground Plane Configuration

While RF radiation from traces on the component and solder sides tend to dominate, there exits a small radiation from the edges at the power-ground planes. King has sugggested following a *20-h rule* in which coupling from the power plane edge tends to terminate better on the ground plane to reduce edge radiation. The concept is illustrated in Fig. 2.13.

Actually, the ending of the power plane around its periphery is small compared to the plane size. For example, for a layer height of 4 mils, the backoff from the periphery edge is 4 mils (0.1 mm) x 20 or 80 mils (2 mm). It is important to remember to back off any signal traces near the edge facing the power plane by an equivalent amount. Also, as explained earlier, no signal trace should be closer than *3 x h* from the board edge.

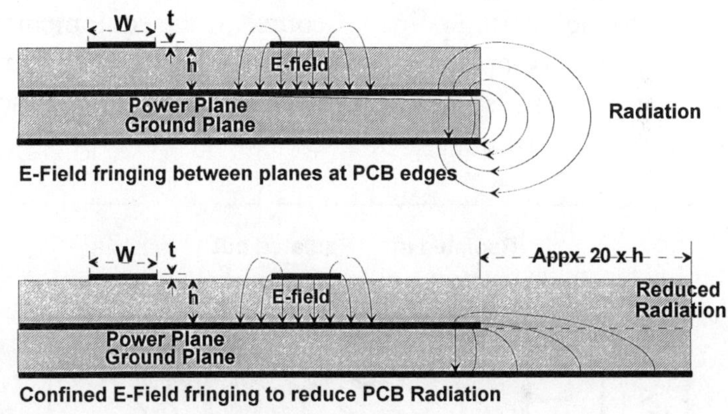


Fig. 2.13 - Illustrating the 20-h rule for reducing edge radiation

## 2.11 Single and Multi-Point Grounding

There is no requirement that the PCB be grounded to an outer conductive housing or chassis to control its EMI performance. It is presumed that tight impedance control practices are in use. Grounding to the chassis at many points may simply offer other *internal* ground loops for current in the ground plane to flow, thereby increasing radiation and crosstalk.

Single-point grounding to the chassis is also not required, although very traditional. It is especially not recommended when the chassis/equipment is inter-connected with one or more other equipments, which derive their own separate power. This can cause loop radiation as shown in Fig. 2.14. By floating (breaking) one or more of the loop contact points, undesired common-mode voltage will be dropped across the resulting capacitance corresponding to the floating point. Of course, if the equipment or module is battery-operated and no battery charger is being used, the problem is greatly deminished. This is discussed further in Chap. 10.

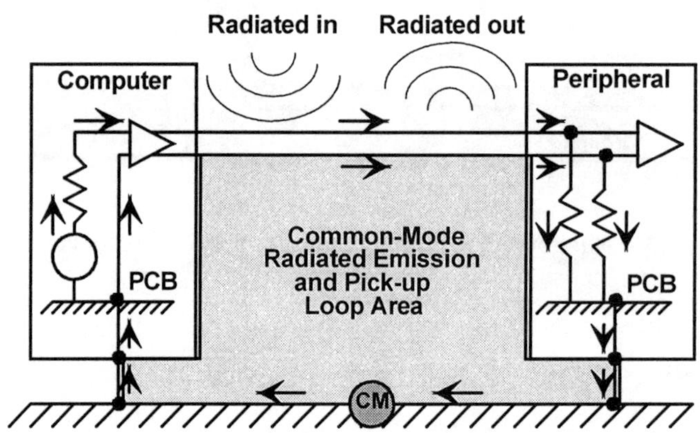


Fig. 2.14 - Interconnected equipments forming ground loops

## 2.12 Logic Families

The correct choice of a logic family is important early in the design stage. Speed, power consumption, noise-immunity level and cost are not the only considerations. From an EMC point-of-view, speed (fast risetime) relates to frequency, and radiated emission is proportional to frequency squared. So, speed is bad news for EMC.

The bandwidth, BW, of logic is defined as the second corner frequency ($F_{02}$) in the Bode plot discussed in Chap. 3:

$$BW = F_{02} = 1/\pi\tau_r \tag{2.6}$$

where, $\tau_r$ is the 10%-90% risetime of the logic family.

The bandwidth includes the clock fundamental frequency, and possibly a few harmonics if the clock is not pushing the logic family speed to the limits. Beyond the bandwidth, the conducted trace current falls off as the square of frequency, or -40 dB/decade. Thus, generalizing, the fundamental and the next nine harmonics of the clock are the principal EMI radiating frequencies of concern.

The noise-immunity level (NIL) is a direct measure of potential EMI susceptibility of a logic family. High-speed CMOS, having NILs of about 1.2 volts, may be contrasted with ECL-10k which has an NIL of about 200 mV. Thus, this CMOS family is 20 $\log_{10}$ (1200/200) or 16 dB less susceptible than ECL-10k. Since CMOS has a lesser bandwidth than ECL, it is further less susceptible.

Table 2.4 lists some of the principal logic in use today or in recent years.

| Table 2.4 - Some principal logic family characteristics | | | | | | |
|---|---|---|---|---|---|---|
| **Logic Family Name** | **Voltage Swing in Volts** | **Rise Time in ns** | **Band-width in MHz** | **Possible Radiation = 5 x BW** | **Input Gate $Z_{in}$ in Ohms** | **Noise Immunity in Volts** |
| ABT-TTL | 3.5 | 3 | 120 | 600 | 75 | 0.6 |
| ACT | 3.5 | 3 | 120 | 600 | 100 | 1.2 |
| ALS-TTL | 3.5 | 3 | 106 | 530 | 435 | 0.5 |
| biCMOS | 3.5 | 10 | 32 | 160 | 100 | 0.4 |
| CMOS-HS | 3.5 | 10 | 32 | 160 | 100 | 0.4 |
| ECL-10kH | 2.5 | 1 | 315 | 1,575 | 50 | 0.7 |
| ECL-100k | 2.5 | 0.7 | 455 | 2,275 | 50 | 0.7 |
| ECLinPS[3] | 2.5 | 0.5 | 635 | 3,175 | 50 | 0.7 |
| E-LITE/ECL | 2.5 | 0.25 | 1,250 | 6,250 | 50 | 0.7 |
| FACT-CMOS | 3 | 2 | 160 | 800 | 100 | 0.9 |
| FAST-TTL | 3.5 | 2 | 160 | 800 | 175 | 0.5 |
| GaAs | 3.5 | 0.2 | 1,600 | 8,000 | 100 | 0.6 |
| HCMOS | 3.5 | 4 | 80 | 400 | 875 | 1 |
| LCX-CMOS | 2 | 3.6 | 90 | 450 | 85 | 0.6 |
| LS-TTL | 3.5 | 6 | 55 | 275 | 440 | 0.6 |
| LVC-CMOS | 2 | 3.6 | 90 | 450 | 85 | 0.6 |
| MG-CMOS | 3.5 | 100 | 3 | 15 | 3,500 | 1 |
| Old CMOS | 5 | 50 | 6 | 30 | 1,000 | 1 |
| STTL, Advanc. | 3.5 | 3 | 120 | 600 | 1,000 | 0.3 |
| STTL-HS | 3.5 | 3 | 120 | 600 | 1,000 | 0.3 |
| STTL-Low Pwr. | 3.5 | 3 | 100 | 500 | 1,000 | 0.3 |
| TTL | 3.5 | 10 | 32 | 160 | 1,000 | 0.4 |
| TTL, Low Pwr. | 3.5 | 10 | 32 | 160 | 1,000 | 0.4 |

## 2.13 Noise Budgeting

Noise budgeting is defined as the amount of allowable EMI or noise to assign to the noise-immunity level of a logic family. To ignore this is to design equipment and install it without any regard for potential EMI other than "if it ain't broke, don't fix it."

Seven principal contributions, as applicable, exist to noise budgeting of the NIL rating of a logic family:

(1) Adequate filtering of the SMPS: The $V_{cc}$ from the switcher power supply may contain some residual switching and high-frequency noise.

(2) Wire, cable or bus run from the SMPS to the backplane or motherboard.

(3) Backplane radiation pickup: For motherboards and backplanes, radiation pickup adds to the noise budget.

(4) Adequate decoupling at chips: Significant trace inductance does not permit providing energy for fast switching, which is provided by the decoupling caps.

(5) PCB ground-loop pickup: Ground-loops on the PCB act as *pickup antennas* to noise sources and EMI.

(6) Crosstalk on PCB: Adjacent traces couple undesired noise from the source trace to the victim trace.

(7) Ground bounce: A condition in which high-speed logic currents and EMI/ESD cause a noise voltage to develop between points due to the finite impedance of a ground plane.

Unless some prorating scheme is used, divide the noise-immunity level of any logic family into seven equal parts. The budgeted noise for each is 14% of the total NIL. For example, for CMOS-HS logic family, with an NIL of 400 mV, budget 57 mV to each of the above seven sources. The more careful designer may wish to budget more noise for bigger sources, such as 100 mV for ground bounce.

## 2.14 References:

Dockey, R. W. and German, R. F. "New Techniques for Reducing Printed Circuit Board Common-Mode Radiation," *IEEE International EMC Symposium,* Dallas, Texas, August 9-13, 1993, pp. 334-339.

Drewniak, J. L.; Hubing, T. H. and Van Doren, T. P., Investigation of Fundamental Mechanisms of Common-Mode Radiation from PCB with Attached Cables, *IEEE International EMC Symposium,* Dallas, Texas, August 9-13, 1993, pp. 334-339.,

German, R. F., Ott, H. W. and Paul, C. R. "Effect of an Image Plane on Printed Circuit Board Radiation," *IEEE International Symposium on Electromagnetic Compatibility,* Washington, D.C., August 21-23, 1990, pp. 284-291.

Heike, R., "EMC Controlled PCB Design," Conference record of the EMC EXPO, *Interference Control Technologies, Inc.,* 1989.

Hill, R. L.; VanDoren, T.; Hubling, T.; and Drewniak, Y. "Common-Mode Currents Induced on Wires Attached to Multi-Layer, Printed-Wire Boards with Segmented Ground Planes," *IEEE International Symposium on Electromagnetic Compatibility,* Chicago, Illinois, August 22-26, 1994, pp. 116-120.

King, W. Michael, discussions within the EMC community.

Mardiguian, M. "Controlling Radiated Emissions by Design," *Van Nostrand Reinhold,* 1992.

Montrose, M. I., "Overview of Design Techniques for Printed Circuit Board Layout Used in High-Technology Products," *IEEE International Symposium on Electromagnetic Compatibility, 1991.*

Montrose, M. I. "Printed Circuit Board Design Techniques for EMC Compliance," *IEEE Press,* 1995.

Paul, C. R. and Bush, D., "Radiated EMI from Common-Mode Currents," *IEEE International symposium on Electromagnetic Compatibility,* Atlanta, 1987.

White, Donald , "EMI Control in the Design of Printed Circuit Boards and Backplanes," *Don White Consultants, Inc.,* 1982.

# Chapter 3

# Predicting PCB Radiation

This chapter addresses the EMI radiation prediction process. Bode plots of conducted trace signal amplitude vs. frequency are given. Then, the radiation from traces combines with the conducted signal amplitudes to produce the field strength at a specified distance. Results are compared with regulatory limits to permit determining performance shortfall. *What-if* exercises are carried out to optimize design or synthesize the required shielding of the PCB external housing.

## 3.1 The EMI Radiation Prediction Process

Predicting EMI radiation is actually a simple process. It is the combination of a number of mathematical models discussed in Volume 8 of the EMC handbook series, "EMI Control Methodology and Procedures" and implemented in the software included with this handbook, if that option was selected.

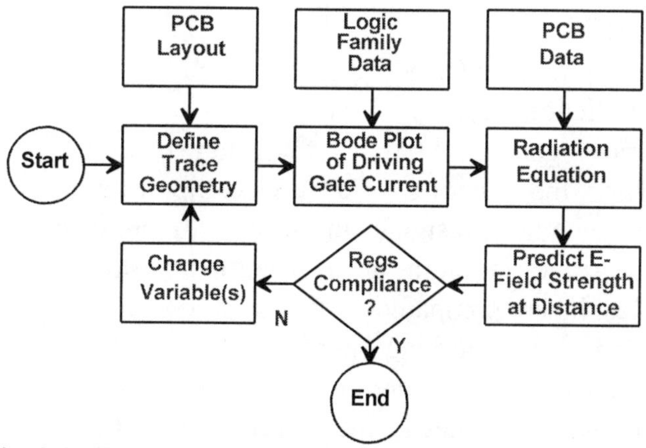


Fig. 3.1 - Flow diagram of radiation prediction process

Figure 3.1 shows the EMI radiation prediction process. Select the logic family and define the trial PCB board layout. Then, compute the Bode plot of conducted IC interconnect trace current vs. frequency. Using the radiation equation, compute the electric-field strength at the regulatory distance normalized to three meters. Compare this field strength with the regulations or objectives. If shortfall, change one or more variables and reiterate the prediction process until the objective is achieved or call this the required box housing shielding effectiveness. If over-designed, relax the PCB board parameters until the object-tive is achieved.

## 3.2 Bode Plots of Clock and Data Line Current

The clock and data waveshape are defined in the time domain and the signal-trace conducted current vs. frequency are defined in the frequency domain. The resultant graph is called a Bode plot.

Figure 3.2 shows the current amplitude, pulse duration and risetime in the frequency domain converted to the current spectral density vs. frequency. Note the first corner frequency, $F_{01}$, in which the slope changes from 0 dB/decade to -20 dB/decade:

$$F_1 = 1/ \ = \text{first corner frequency} \qquad (3.1)$$

and, the second corner frequency, $F_2$, in which the slope changes from -20 dB/decade to -40 dB/decade

$$F_2 = 1/ = \text{second corner frequency} \qquad (3.2)$$

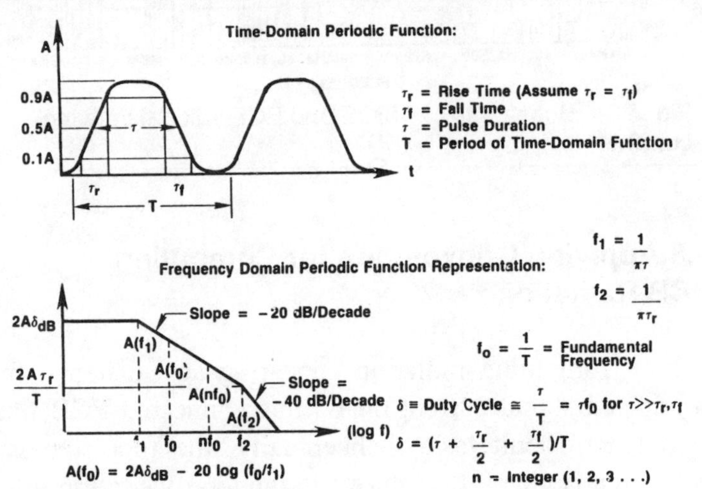


Fig. 3.2 - Geometry for Bode plots

Figure 3.3 shows the application of the Bode plots to CMOS (voltage swing = 3.5 volts and risetime = 10 nsec) and ECL-10k (voltage swing = 0.8 volts and risetime = 2 nsec). In the former case the clock frequency assumed was 10 MHz and for the ECL-10k, the clock was 50 MHz. Note the crossover in amplitude above about 15 MHz.

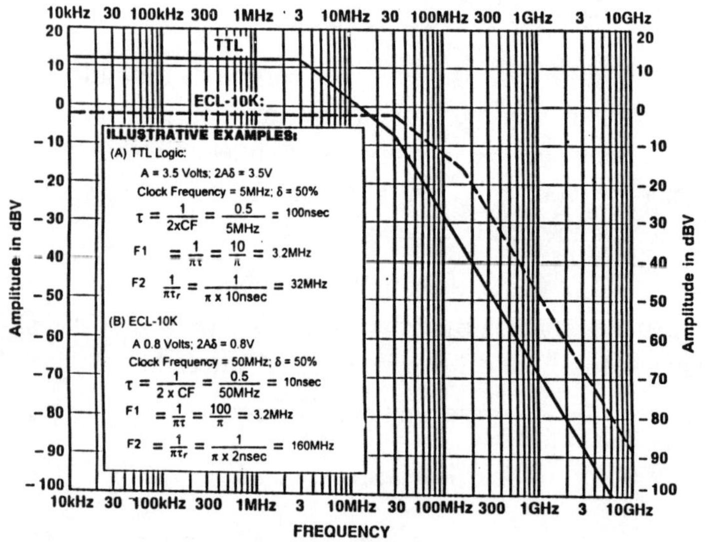


Fig. 3.3 - Bode plots of CMOS and ECL-10k gate driving currents

## 3.3 Applying Convolution for Computing PCB Radiation

Computing radiation appearing at a distance from conducted signal current on IC interconnected PCB traces is not a difficult task. Conceptually, the first step is to perform a Bode plot, as shown in the top illustration in Fig.

3.4. This is the envelope of the harmonic conducted emission current to the driven gate from a driving gate trace. Note the two corner frequencies and the three slopes of current in the envelope. From the wave equation, the far-field component is plotted in the center illustration. Note its break frequency at a half wavelength above which radiation increases with frequency (+20 dB/dec) rather than the square of frequency (+40 dB/dec).

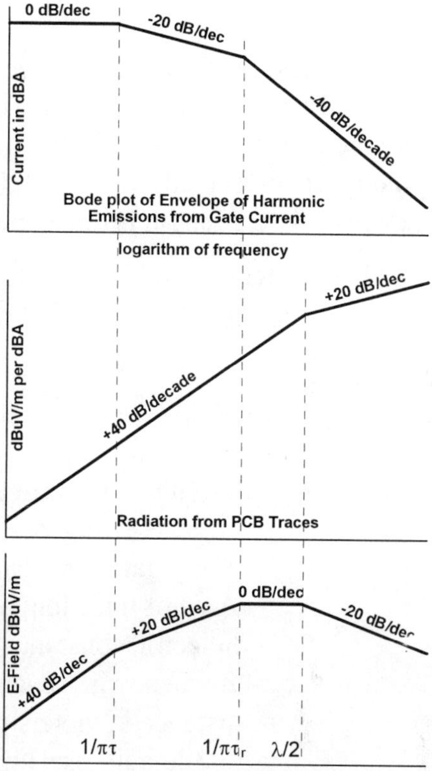


Fig. 3.4 - Convolution of trace gate current and trace radiation to produce electric field at a distance

By adding the slopes and their values from the top and center illustrations, the bottom plot results. This produces three corner frequencies and four slopes. The region captioned *"0 dB/decade"* corresponds to the highest radiation level and is where the radiated emission noncompliance with applicable regulations is most likely to exist. Note: this exists between the logic bandwidth and the frequency corresponding to a half wavelength of the average trace length.

## 3.4 Radiation from a Single Trace Circuit

The far-field radiation equation is given in reference (1) and several other sources. To facilitate discussion here, a single driving gate - driven gate interconnect trace geometry is presented in Fig. 3.5. From this, the radiated electric-field strength is developed:

Radiated Electric-Field Strength:

$$E_{dBuV/m} = 20 \log_{10}(263 \times 10^{-7} I_{mA} A_{mm2} f^2_{MHz}/r_m) \text{ dBuV/m}, \quad (3.3)$$

$$\text{for } L_{mm} < \lambda/2\sqrt{\varepsilon_r}$$

$$= 20 \log_{10}[1.75 \times 10^{-7} I_{mA} h_{mm} f_{MHz}/(r_m \sqrt{\varepsilon_r})] \quad (3.4)$$

$$\text{for } L_{mm} > \lambda/2\sqrt{\varepsilon_r}$$

where, $I_{mA}$ = Driving gate current in mA
= Voltage Swing/$Z_{in}$
$Z_{in}$ = input gate impedance in ohms
$A_{mm}$ = Area of trace loop in $mm^2$ = $L_{mm}$ x $h_{mm}$
$\varepsilon_r$ = dielectric constant = appx. 3-4 (typically)
$f_{MHz}$ = frequency in MHz
$r_m$ = distance in meters per applicable regulation (default, use 3 m; see Chap.1)

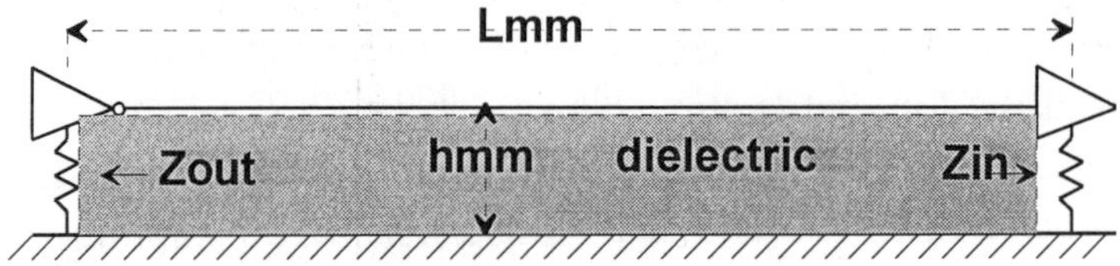


Fig. 3.5 - Single driving and driven gate with interconnect trace

### *Illustrative Example:*

First, calculate the radiation from a 40 MHz single driving-driven gate interconnected with a trace run of 10 cm. The PCB board has a layer thickness of 0.25 mm (10 mils) and a dielectric constant of 4.0. The logic family is ACT which has a risetime of 3 nsec, a 3.5 volt swing and an input impedance of 100 ohms. Compute the radiation level at a three-meter distance and compare it with FCC R&R, Part 15.B, Class B limits.

The problem will be solved in two parts:

(1) Develop the Bode Plot for the driven gate current harmonics vs. frequency from 40 MHz to 1000 MHz.

(2) Calculate the radiated field strength vs. frequency and compare with the regulation limits.

Figure 3.6 is the application of the procedure of Fig. 3.4 to develop the amplitudes of the ACT driven gate current fundamental and harmonic frequencies of 40 MHz. The fundamental is calculated below.

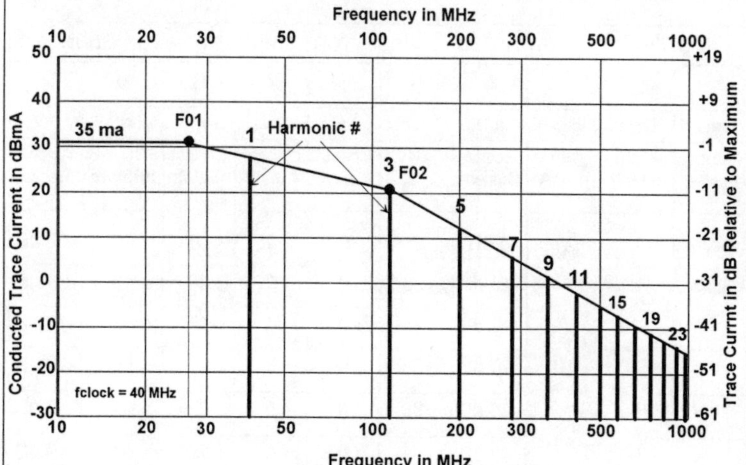


Fig. 3.6 - Bode plot of envelope of conducted trace current

ACT Logic: $V_{swing} = 3.5$ volts. $f_{clock} = 40$ MHz. $\tau_r = 3$ nsec.
$Z_{in}$ = input gate impedance = 100 ohms. $\varepsilon_r = 4.0$
$L_{mm} = 100$ mm. $h_{mm} = 0.25$ mm. $A_{mm2} = 25\ mm^2$
$f_{01} = 2f_{clock}/\pi = 25.5$ MHz. $f_{02} = 1/\pi\tau_r = 106$ MHz
$I_{mA} = 1000 \times 3.5/100$ ohms = 35 mA = 31 dBmA.
$I_{40MHz} = 35 \times (26/40) = 22.3$ mA = 27 dBmA. r = 3 m
$E_{dBuV/m} = 20\log_{10}(263\times10^{-7}*22*25*40^2/3)$ dBuV/m,
for $f_{MHz} < 750$ MHz ($L_{mm} < \lambda/2\sqrt{\varepsilon_r}$)
$= 20\log_{10}(7.7) = 18$ dBuV/m

By applying the above relations and Fig. 3.6 several times to different clock harmonic numbers (first column), Tab. 3.1 results. The computed E-Field is shown in the eighth column. The sixth and seventh columns are 0 dB since fanout and number of traces are both = 1. The ninth column lists the FCC radiation limits at a 3-m distance for Class B (product locations = residential. See Chap. 1 for limits). The last column (10th) is the dB by which the trace-loop radiations are above or below the FCC limits.

Table 3.1 - Computed E-fields from single trace radiation

| 1 | 2 | 3 | 4 | 5 | 6 | 7 | 8 | 9 | 10 |
|---|---|---|---|---|---|---|---|---|---|
| Data | Data | Fig. 3.6 | Fig. 3.6 | Comput | Data | Data | 18+4+5 | Data | 8-9 |
| Harmon. Number | Freq. in MHz | Curr. dBmA | Relatv. Current | $(f_{MH}/40)^2$ in dB | Fanout # in dB | Traces # in dB | E-Field dBuV/m | FCC15B dBuV/m | Above Below |
| Fundam | 40 | 27 | 0 dB | 0 | 0 | 0 | 18 | 40 | -22 dB |
| 3rd | 120 | See Fig. 3.6 | -10 dB | +20 | 0 | 0 | 28 | 43 | -15 dB |
| 5th | 200 | | -19 dB | +28 | 0 | 0 | 27 | 43 | -16 dB |
| 7th | 280 | | -25 dB | +34 | 0 | 0 | 27 | 46 | -19 dB |
| 9th | 360 | | -29 dB | +38 | 0 | 0 | 27 | 46 | -19 dB |
| 19th | 760 | | -42 dB | +51 | 0 | 0 | 27 | 46 | -19 dB |
| 25th | 1,000 | | -47 dB | +51 | 0 | 0 | 22 | 46 | -24 dB |

An examination of Tab. 3.1 shows that worst case radiation occurs at the 3rd harmonic (120 MHz) of the clock, where radiation is 15 dB below the limits for a single trace.

## 3.5 Composite PCB Radiation

In the preceding section the computed radiation is from a single trace-loop area only. Since the overall or composite radiations are sought for an entire PCB, it is necessary to include (1) the average fanout (fanout is the number of driven gates by a single driving gate), rather than a fanout of one assumed in Tab. 3.1 in the single-trace radiation and (2) the effect of all traces located outside the internal power-ground planes on the component and solder sides of the PCBs. If the average fanout were now two, then the values in column six of Tab. 3.1 would be 6 dB higher as shown in Tab. 3.2.

Table 3.2 - Computed radiation from total PCB radiation

| 1 | 2 | 3 | 4 | 5 | 6 | 7 | 8 | 9 | 10 |
|---|---|---|---|---|---|---|---|---|---|
| Data | Data | Fig3.6 | Fig.3.6 | Comput | Data | Data | 64+4+5 | Data | 8-9 |
| Hamon number | Freq. in MHz | Curr. dBmA | Relatv. Curren | $(f_{MH}/40)^2$ in dB | Fanout # in dB | Traces # in dB | E-Field dBuV/ | FCC15B dBuV/m | Above Below |
| Fundam | 40 | 27 | 0 dB | 0 | 6 | 40 | 64 | 40 | +24dB |
| 3rd | 120 | | -10 dB | +20 | 6 | 40 | 74 | 43 | +31dB |
| 5th | 200 | See Fig. 3.6 | -19 dB | +28 | 6 | 40 | 73 | 43 | +30dB |
| 7th | 280 | | -25 dB | +34 | 6 | 40 | 73 | 46 | +27dB |
| 9th | 360 | | -29 dB | +38 | 6 | 40 | 73 | 46 | +27dB |
| 19th | 760 | | -42 dB | +51 | 6 | 40 | 73 | 46 | +27dB |
| 25th | 1,000 | | -47 dB | +51 | 6 | 40 | 68 | 46 | +22dB |

If there were 100 such interconnect traces, then 40 dB is added in column 7 to show that the worst case in column 10 is now = +31 dB out of compliance at the frequency of the third harmonic rather than 15 dB, as shown before. The number "64" in column 8 represents the addition of 6 dB + 40 dB to Tab. 3.1 "18 dB."

One departing note: the above analysis does not include any common-mode radiation from the I/O cable. This is performed in Chap. 10. Cable radiation from common-mode current is another software program appearing in the floppy disk.

## 3.6 Running Radiation Software Program #3800

If the reader has purchased the software which is intended to be used with this book (that was an option when the book was purchased), remove it now from the pocket inside the back cover. If the software was not purchased, skip this section and go to Chap. 4. If the reader would like to license the software for $185, call 540-347-0030.

Insert the disk into your A (or B) drive. Under *Program Manager* in Windows™, select *File, Run.* Then type a:\emc-engr\setup (or a:\startkit\setup) and execute *Enter.* You may also want to transfer the EMC Buyers' Guide (a:\buy-guid\setup) onto your hard drive, as well. This will allow you to browse the program for the EMC products directory and their suppliers.

Select the icon for EMC-ENGR in your *Program Manager* screen. You will see the screen shown in Fig. 3.7.

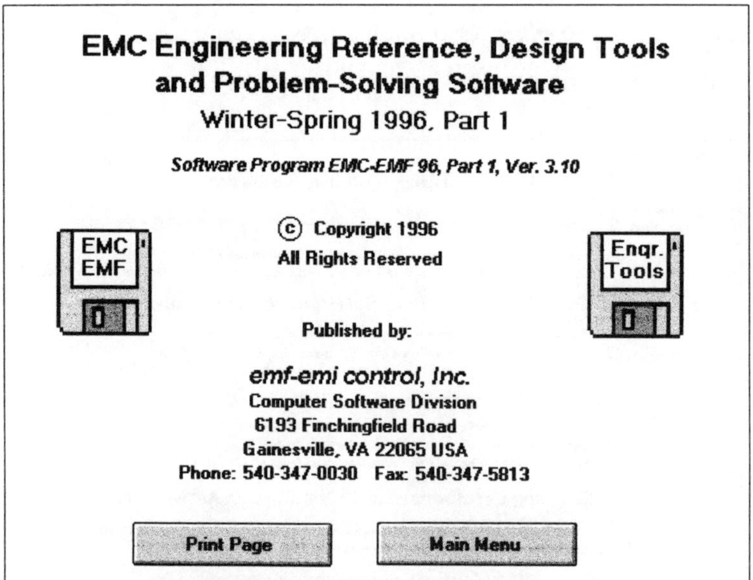


Fig. 3.7 - Cover page

Click on *Main Menu* to see the screen in Fig. 3.8.

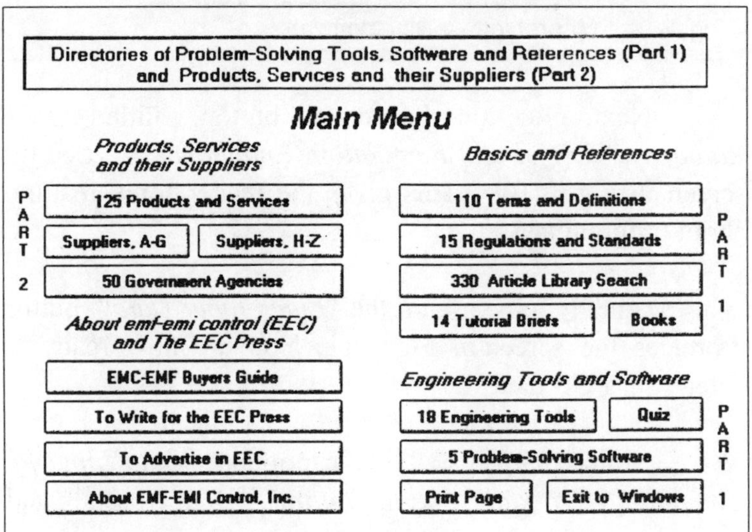


Fig. 3.8 - Main menu

Then select (click) on *"Problem-Solving Software"* which will display the screen shown in Fig. 3.9.

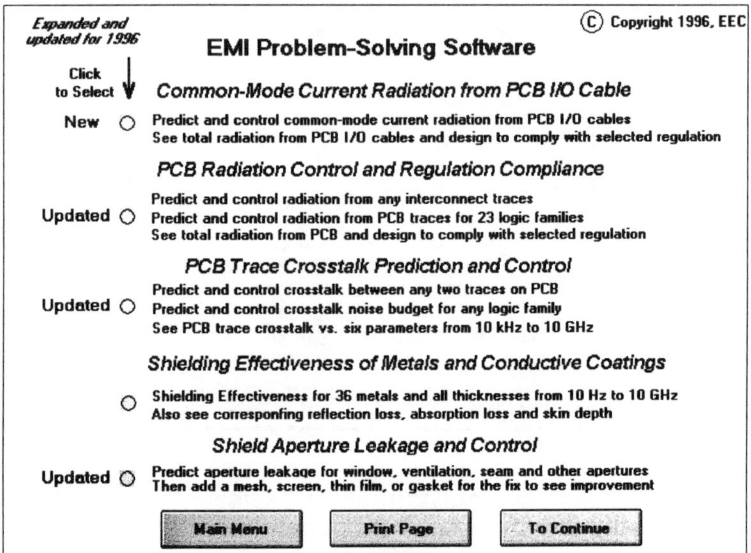


Fig. 3.9 - EMI problem-solving software

Next, click on the second button entitled *"PCB Radiation Control and Regulation Compliance"*. See the screen in Fig. 3.10. This gives the reader some features about program #3800.

Finally, clicking on the *"Enter Input Data"* button produces the screen in Fig. 3.11. You are now ready to enter your PCB data.

Notice that Fig. 3.11 is captioned *"Data Input for Computing Crosstalk and Radiation"*. Both crosstalk and

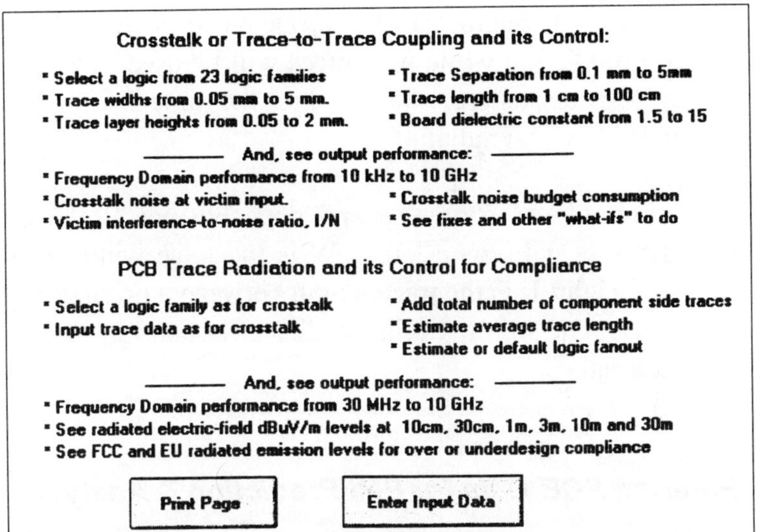


Fig. 3.10 - Overview and features of program #3800

radiation are shown since they use about 80% of the same data. The figure shows a 3-D view of two traces above a

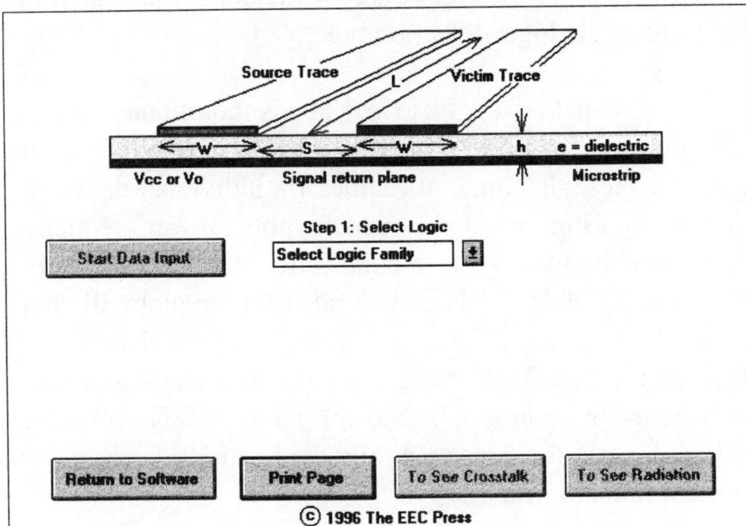


3.11 - Data input for computing crosstalk and radiation

ground plane in microstrip. Only one trace is needed for radiation prediction while two traces will be used in a later chapter for crosstalk prediction. For the time being, the program focuses on radiation.

Figure 3.11 shows several data, but not all, to be entered. More will come later. W is the trace width; h is the layer height; L is the trace length between a driving and driven gate; and e is the relative dielectric constant of the layer material.

## *Entering PCB Data for EMI Prediction & Analysis*

The first step is to select the logic family. Clicking on the down arrow produces a list of 23 logic families for selection. In the example, ACT has been chosen (clicked) as shown in Fig. 3.12. Six data for this family are shown to the right of the logic-selection box.

The next step is to select six additional data by clicking on *"Start Data Input"* box. The program requires entering these data, one at a time, via individual data entry questions from windows which pop up in sequence. Although frequency is included for the purpose of a forthcoming table display, the final radiation plot will cover from 30 MHz to 10 GHz. One example of the data display is shown in Fig. 3.13. Note, the data for trace separation is only relevant to crosstalk and the word *"common"* means actual length for non-crosstalk applications such as the present radiation focus.

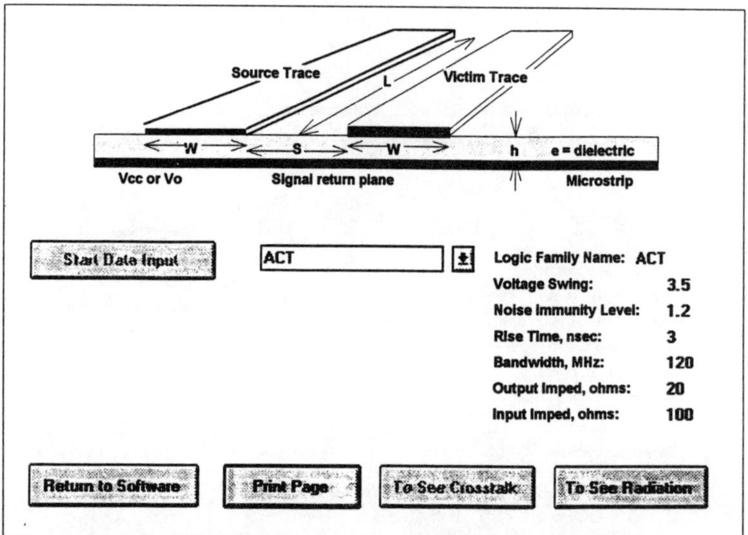


Fig. 3.12 - Data input for computing crosstalk and radiation

If any of the data (including logic family) selected is not correct, simply click on the logic family down arrow or *"Start Data Input,"* as applicable. When all data are correct, click on *"To See Radiation."* Then, Fig. 3.14 appears.

The table may be scrolled down and to the right to reveal frequencies from 10 kHz to 10 GHz and radiation distances from 10 cm to 30 meters corresponding to the inputted data shown at the bottom of the table. Clicking on *"See Radiation Plot"* sends the user to the next screen shown in Fig. 3.15. Note that there are three more data to be entered. Focus attention on the number of traces on the component side above the power plane and on the solder side below the ground plane. Estimate their average trace length corresponding to 50% of their population and input

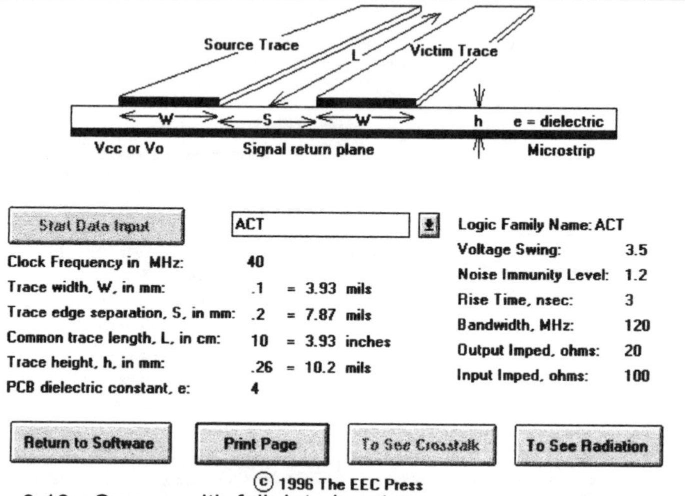

Fig. 3.13 - Screen with full data input

this length in cm. Estimate (or count) the corresponding number of traces and input this. Finally, estimate the average fanout or number of driven gates by a driving gate.

| Frequency | 30 cm | 50 cm | 70 cm | 1 m | 2 m | 3 m | 5 m | 7 m | 10 m | 20 m | 30 m | Freq |
|---|---|---|---|---|---|---|---|---|---|---|---|---|
| 1 MHz | 22 | 13 | 7 | 1 | -11 | -17 | -26 | -31 | -37 | -48 | -54 | 1 |
| 1.5 MHz | 26 | 17 | 11 | 5 | -7 | -14 | -22 | -27 | -33 | -43 | -49 | 1.5 |
| 2 MHz | 28 | 19 | 14 | 8 | -4 | -11 | -19 | -24 | -30 | -40 | -45 | 2 |
| 3 MHz | 32 | 23 | 17 | 11 | 0 | -7 | -15 | -20 | -25 | -34 | -39 | 3 |
| 5 MHz | 36 | 28 | 22 | 16 | 5 | -2 | -9 | -14 | -19 | -27 | -32 | 5 |
| 7 MHz | 39 | 31 | 25 | 19 | 8 | 2 | -5 | -10 | -14 | -22 | -26 | 7 |
| 10 MHz | 43 | 34 | 29 | 23 | 12 | 6 | -1 | -5 | -9 | -17 | -21 | 10 |
| 15 MHz | 46 | 38 | 33 | 27 | 17 | 11 | 5 | 1 | -3 | -10 | -14 | 15 |
| 20 MHz | 49 | 41 | 36 | 30 | 20 | 15 | 9 | 5 | 1 | -5 | -9 | 20 |
| 30 MHz | 52 | 44 | 39 | 33 | 24 | 19 | 14 | 10 | 7 | 0 | -4 | 30 |
| 50 MHz | 53 | 45 | 40 | 35 | 27 | 23 | 17 | 14 | 10 | 4 | 0 | 50 |
| 70 MHz | 53 | 46 | 42 | 37 | 29 | 25 | 20 | 16 | 13 | 7 | 3 | 70 |
| 100 MHz | 54 | 48 | 43 | 39 | 32 | 27 | 22 | 19 | 16 | 10 | 6 | 100 |
| 150 MHz | 53 | 46 | 43 | 39 | 31 | 28 | 23 | 20 | 16 | 10 | 7 | 150 |
| 200 MHz | 52 | 46 | 42 | 38 | 31 | 27 | 23 | 20 | 16 | 10 | 7 | 200 |
| 300 MHz | 50 | 45 | 41 | 37 | 31 | 27 | 22 | 19 | 16 | 10 | 7 | 300 |
| 500 MHz | 49 | 44 | 40 | 37 | 31 | 27 | 22 | 19 | 16 | 10 | 7 | 500 |
| 700 MHz | 48 | 43 | 40 | 37 | 30 | 27 | 22 | 19 | 16 | 10 | 7 | 700 |
| 1 GHz | 48 | 43 | 40 | 37 | 30 | 27 | 22 | 19 | 16 | 10 | 7 | 1 |

Logic Family: ACT
Trace width in mm: .1
Trace separation in mm: .2
Trace height in mm: .26
Trace Length in cm: 10
Dielectric constant: 4

Return to Data Input | Print Page | See Radiation Plot

Fig. 3.14 - Table of radiation from traces in dBuV/m

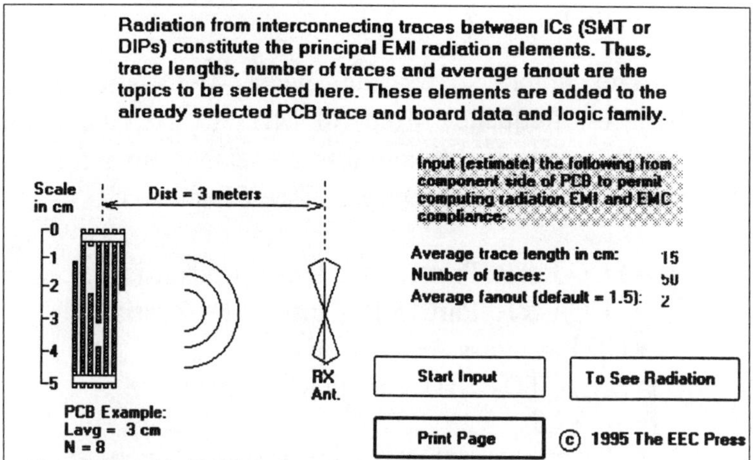


Fig. 3.15 - Final PCB data to be entered

When these data have been entered, click on *"To See Radiation."* The results of radiation level vs. frequency

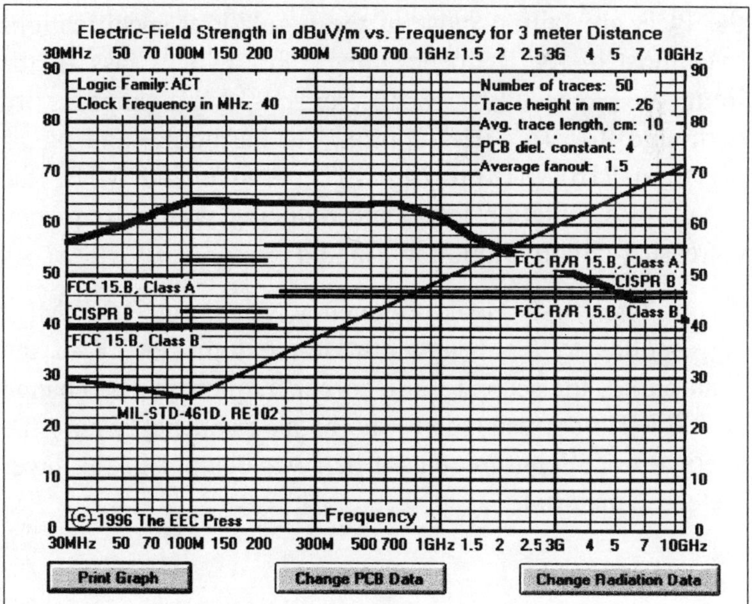


Fig. 3.16 - Plot of electric field vs. frequency

are shown in Fig. 3.16.

The graph shows the electric-field strength in dBuV/m vs. frequency from 30 MHz to 10 GHz. Four regulation or specification limits are also shown for performance compliance comparison (see Chapter 1):

- FCC R&R, Part 15.B, Class A (industrial)
- FCC R&R, Part 15.B, Class B (residential).
- CISPR, Class B
- MIL-STD-461D, Limits RE-102

For reference, the previously inputted logic and trace data are shown in the upper left and upper right in the graph.

Figure 3.16 shows that the radiated emissions from the PCB are failing most of the regulations/specifications over most of the frequency range. For FCC, Class B, the limits are exceeded by 18 dB from 100 MHz (approx. 3rd harmonic) to 216 MHz (approx. 5th harmonic) and by 15 dB from 216 MHz to 700 MHz. Above 700 MHz, the out-of-spec radiation levels are reducing with a frequency increase. (cf. convolution in Fig. 3.4).

The first break frequency at about 100 MHz corresponds to the bandwidth of the logic (ACT in the example) or the second Bode corner frequency. The change at 700 MHz corresponds to the break frequency where the average trace length equals a half wavelength in the layer dielectric material.

### *Exercising the Design Data for the Fix*

Note, it is possible that you may eventually get a screen notice to input your code number, if that happens, input it now or call 540-347-0030 for more information.

As observed from the graph plot above, the radiations are 18 dB above the FCC limit at the third harmonic of the clock. Now comes the fix. Either the trace radiations must be reduced or this failure used as a basis for adding an external shielded box housing.

First, recognize that any EMI prediction process has errors estimated to be under 8 dB, and that EMI compliance measurement equipment and procedures also have errors estimated to average 6 dB (see references). Failure to know

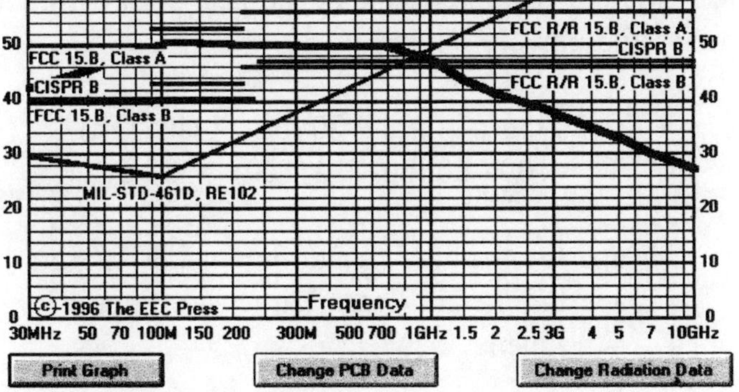


Fig. 3.17 - Rerun - plot of electric field vs. frequency for 2 mil layer height

or acknowledge that measurement errors exist, is not living in the real world. Thus, a recommended 10-dB "safety margin" is recommended for the 18-dB, out of compliance in the example, to produce a 28-dB reduction requirement.

A 28 dB is too large a disparity to try to reduce multilayer PCB radiations. Even if the trace height were reduced from 10 mils to 2 mils, as typical for PCMCIA cards, the improvement would only be $20 \log_{10}(10/2) = 14$ dB. Fig. 3.17 is a rerun based on this change.

It is possible to consider outer ground planes placed over the component and solder sides. If half of the IC interconnect traces are on either side, the solder side plane would reduce radiations by 6 dB, but the component side would have to have broached holes to clear the higher SMT (surface-mount technology) components. An additional improvement here is based on the resulting aperture leakage, which is one of the other software programs (Program #3600) included with the disk.

If the cleared SMT component produces an aperture of one cm, the resulting leakage at 120 MHz (third harmonic) would be:

$$SE_{dB} = 100 - 20 \log_{10}(Lf_{MHz}) + 20 \log_{10}(1+\ln_e(L/h) \qquad (3.5)$$
$$= 100 - 20 \log_{10}(10*120) = 38 \text{ dB}$$

where, L is aperture length (greater dimension) in mm
h is aperture height (lesser dimension) in mm
$f_{MHz}$ = frequency in MHz

One conclusion is that ground planes on both sides of the PCB can fix the radiation problem and render unnecessary the reduction of layer height. But, it compromises PCB board repair and adds additional cost. This cost, however, may not be as expensive as placing the entire PCB inside of a shielded box housing. Further analysis here is beyond the scope of this book. See Volume 3, *Electromagnetic Shielding,* page vi of this book.

## 3.8 References

Dockey, R.W. and German, R.F., New Techniques for Reducing Printed Circuit Board Common-Mode Radiation," *IEEE International EMC Symposium,* Dallas Texas, August 9-13, 1993, pp. 334-339.

German, R.F.; Ott, H.; and Paul, C.R., "Effect of an Image Plane on Printed Circuit Board Radiation," *IEEE International Symposium on Electromagnetic Compatibility,* Wash. D.C., August 21-23, 1990, pp. 284-291.

Heinke, R., "EMC Controlled PCB Design," Conference Record of the EMC EXPO, *Interference Control Technologies, Inc.,* 1989.

Mardiguian, M., "Controlling Radiated Emissions by Design," *Van Nostrand Reinhold*, 1992.

Montrose, M.I., "Overview of Design Techniques for Printed Circuit Board Layout Used in High-Technology Products," *IEEE International Symposium on Electromagnetic Compatibility,* 1991

Paul, C.R. and Bush, D., "Radiated EMI from Common-Mode Currents," *IEEE International Symposium on Electromagnetic Compatibility*, Atlanta, 1987

White, Donald R.J. White, "EMI Controlling the Design of Printed Circuit Boards and Backplanes," *Don White Consultants, Inc.,* 1982.

Volume 8, Handbook Series on Electromagnetic Interference and Compatibility, "EMI Control Methodology and Procedures," *The EEC Press.*

# Chapter 4

# Power Distribution and Bussing

This chapter addresses D-C power distribution from the source (usually a switching-mode power supply) to the end use (a switching gate and a driven gate). For rack-mounted equipment, this can be a one-meter concatenation of handovers from source to load with intervening points or areas where EMI can enter or exit. For a simple multilayer board, power distribution is only from the input of a power-ground plane to the surface-mounted ICs. But, even for this, decoupling capacitor selection, sizing and mounting can give poor EMI performance if not done correctly.

## 4.1 Power Distribution Concatenation

Figure 4.1 illustrates the different stages of power distribution and handover in an equipment or rack-mounted subsystem. The distance from the switcher to the consuming IC gates may be a meter or more. For no SMPS and backplanes (e.g. PCMCIA cards), the input may be a DC/DC converter and the gates may be only a few cm away.

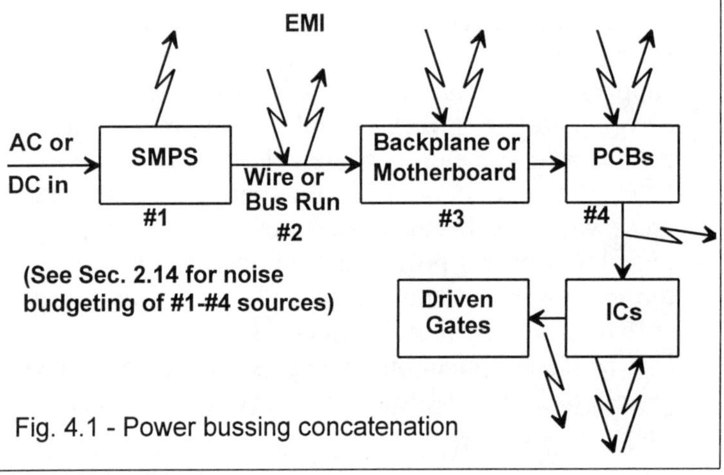


Fig. 4.1 - Power bussing concatenation

Figure 4.1 also illustrates the many locations along the power distribution path that EMI can enter and/or exit. The switcher is electrically noisy and both conducts and radiates EMI. Its output H-F decoupling cap may not be performing because of too low a self-resonant frequency. This resonant frequency should exist above the logic bandwidth ($1/\pi\tau_r$).

The run from the switcher (especially if located in the bottom of the equipment rack) to the backplane may be a meter and is a long path for EMI to enter and/or exit. Twisting wiring distribution will have no effect on common-mode radiation or pickup.

Unless shielded, the backplane also represents EMI opportunities for radiation and pickup. Microstrip interconnect traces using the power-distribution backplane will share their signal returns with EMI to partially consume their logic noise-immunity budgets (see Sec. 2.14). The same will happen to a lesser extent on the individual PCBs, which also require bulk and R-F bypass caps on the inside of their edge connectors. At the IC and chip level, EMC performance will depend upon the proper sizing, location and self-resonant properties of the decoupling capacitance's, discussed in later sections.

Thus, in general, the $V_{CC}$ and $V_0$ wire or bus distribution system consists of a number of *antenna-like* components which can significantly degrade the overall EMC properties ranging from consuming noise budgets to contaminating other logic performance. Unfortunately, the designer rarely attempts to measure, compute or allocate noise budgets for this, resulting in a largely unknown performance viz., *if the system works, don't worry about it.*

## 4.2 Power Distribution on Single-Layer Boards

Opportunities for EMI radiation and pickup are especially pronounced for double-sided, single-layer boards (SLB). Fig. 4.2 shows a typical illustration of a signal and power trace distribution system for SLBs. Notice the many loops existing from a DIP or SMT to other ICs and return.

Since the $V_{CC}$ and $V_0$ traces also contain R-F noise as well as DC, their radiation and pickup is proportional to their corresponding loop areas:

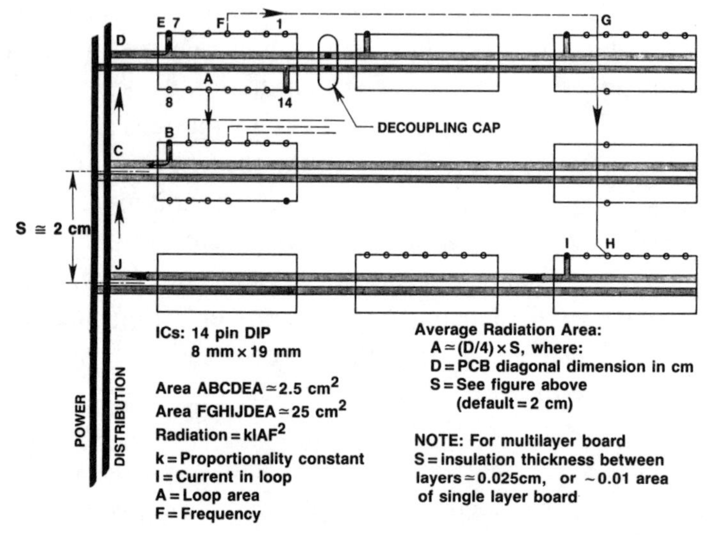


Fig. 4.2 - Signal and power trace distribution in single-layer boards

$$\text{Radiation from loops} = k_1\, IAf^2 \text{ for } L<\lambda/2 \qquad (4.1)$$

$$\text{Radiation into loops} = k_2\, EAf \text{ for } L<\lambda/2 \qquad (4.2)$$

where, $k_1$ and $k_2$ are obtained from the radiation or wave equations (see Chap. 3).

I = the fundamental and harmonic current from the logic gate toggling action

E = ambient electric-field strength appearing at the loop areas

A= trace loop areas = L x h

L = larger dimension of the loop areas

h = smaller dimension of the loop areas
f = frequency
λ = wavelength corresponding to f:

$$\lambda_m = 300/f_{MHz} \tag{4.3}$$

As they develop, the loop areas of double-sided, SLBs are typically one to two orders of magnitude greater than the equivalent loop areas on multilayer boards. Thus, their radiation into and out of these loops will be 20 to 40 dB greater than radiation from multilayer boards. Similarly, since crosstalk is proportional to these loop areas as well, crosstalk will be correspondingly worse for SLBs.

Figure 2.7 in Chap. 2 previously discussed how the loop areas can be reduced in SLBs by the use of a phantom image plane located just below the solder side of a SLB.

Raised power bussing was frequently used in SLB during the 1980s to help reduce the above areas and to reduce trace voltage drop because of power regulation problems. Raised power bussing is rarely used today. However, since then, nearly all PCBs have gone the multilayer board route.

## 4.3 Power Distribution on Multi-Layer Boards

As explained in Chap. 2 on multilayer boards (MLB), the power plane and signal-return plane form a low-impedance, power-distribution system for the PCB. As discussed earlier in Tab. 2.3, the characteristic impedance of this power bussing is of the order of 0.1 to 1 ohm. This is contrasted with 10-300 ohms for SLBs - approximately two orders of magnitude poorer for SLBs. The only redeeming feature of power distribution for SLBs seems to be that much lower-speed logic families are used in SLB design so that their noise-immunity budgeting is less damaged at lower frequencies.

There is a temptation and prevalent practice in MLB design not to face off a $V_{CC}$ power distribution plane with its adjoining $V_0$ return plane, also doubling for signal return. The practice, as discussed in Chap. 2, is to bury one or two signal trace layers between $V_{CC}$ and $V_0$ . This has the perceived value of ensuring that every interconnecting trace is only one layer from its return path (assuming no trace layers are used on the outboard component and/or solder sides). This has certain efficiency values to reduce the number of layers, but at a price of increasing the power distribution impedance by a factor of 2 or 3 and creating increased common-mode currents within the PCBs. Unfortunately, some of these currents couple to the PCB I/O cable which exacerbates cable radiation.

## 4.4 Decoupling Capacitance

The problem, of course, with all PCB power distribution systems is that the self inductance between the points of D-C power generation and consumption is far too large. The resulting impedance makes it necessary to get and store the power at the ICs for their fast toggling consumption. Even the inductance at this point can be debilitating if not properly controlled, as shown in Fig. 4.3.

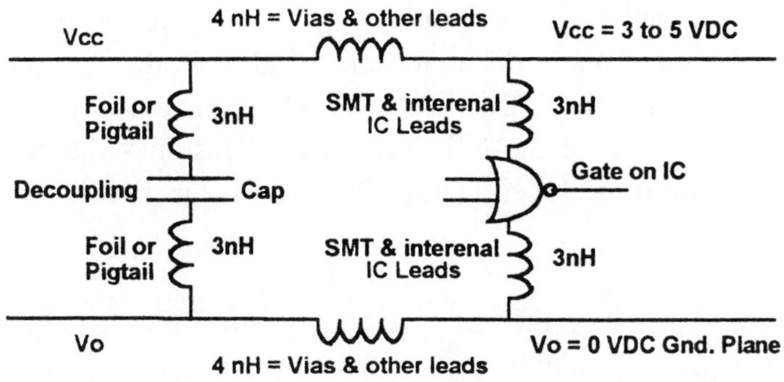


Fig. 4.3 - Parasitic inductance of trace, cap and IC leads

The self inductance of the decoupling-cap leads plus that of the DIPs or their lower-value SMT components plus that of vias (1-2 nH each) may approximate 20 nH. The resulting voltage drop, $V_d$, is:

$$V_d = - LdI/dt \tag{4.4}$$

where, L = the total round-trip path self inductance in nH
dI = the switched gate and driving gate(s) current of he logic family
dt is the logic edge rate or rise time in nsec of the logic family.

As an example, assume the driven gate current of ACT logic approximates 30 mA and its risetime is 3 nsec. For a 20 nH path inductance, Eq. (4.4) becomes:

$$V_d = 20 \times 0.03/3 = 200 \text{ mV}$$

For a total noise-immunity level of 1 volt, and 170 mV assigned as a noise budget to $V_{CC}$ sag (stability), the performance meets the requirement. But, if the fanout is, say four, then the sag is 800 mV, which exceeds the noise budget portion of the NIL and nearly consumes the entire noise-immunity level. Thus, 20 nH is far too high an inductance.

To reduce the path inductance from the decoupling cap to the IC, simply reduce the path length. The best approach, however, is to locate the decoupling cap(s) directly inside the DIPs or SMT components. Many, if not most SMT ICs now provide this.

The minimum capacitance value, $C_d$ of the decoupling cap to service a single gate is:

$$C_d = \frac{I}{dV/dt} \qquad (4.5)$$

I = The toggling gate current plus that of all driven gates from subject gate
dV = voltage swing of the toggling action
dt = logic family edge rate or risetime.

Using the previous example of ACT logic driving a single gate, Eq. (4.5) becomes:

$$C_d = 0.03 /(3.5\text{V}/3\text{nsec})\ \text{nF}$$
$$= 26\ \text{pF}$$

If the decoupling cap is to service 200 total gates including gates on the IC and driven gates on other ICs, the capacitance value is 26 pF x 100 = 2,600 pF, based on 50% of the gates being toggled at any time.

But, examine further to see if the above 2,600 pF cap and its loop inductance of 10 nH will perform as expected. The self-resonant frequency, $f_{res}$ of this installed cap is:

$$f_{res} = 1/2\pi\sqrt{L_d C_d} = 31 \text{ MHz} \quad (4.6)$$

The bandwidth, BW, of the ACT logic family is:

$$BW = 1/\pi\tau_r = 106 \text{ MHz} \quad (4.7)$$

where $\tau_r$ = risetime = 3 nsec.

So, the ACT logic needs at least 100 MHz bandwidth and the self-resonant frequency of the previous example is 31 MHz. Thus, the arrangement won't work (or performs in a much degraded manner) since the cap looks like an inductor above 31 MHz. But, what are the options to fix the problem?

(1) Reduce the cap's loop inductance well below its present 20 nH value in the example. Unless the decoupling cap(s) are built-in to the ICs, further lead inductance reduction may be difficult to achieve.

(2) By-pass the decoupling cap(s) with parallel caps of much less value. For example, shunt the 2,600 pF cap in

the above example with a 100 pF cap. If solderable leadless caps are used (this is a misnomer since the external inductance remains), the self-resonant frequency can be extended above 100 MHz.

Note that there exists a narrow region (high Q) between the two self-resonant frequencies of the caps, where parallel resonance exists. This results from the larger cap appearing as an inductance above its resonant frequency which in turn can resonate with the capacitance of the smaller cap.

Figure 4.4 shows the impedance vs. frequency of

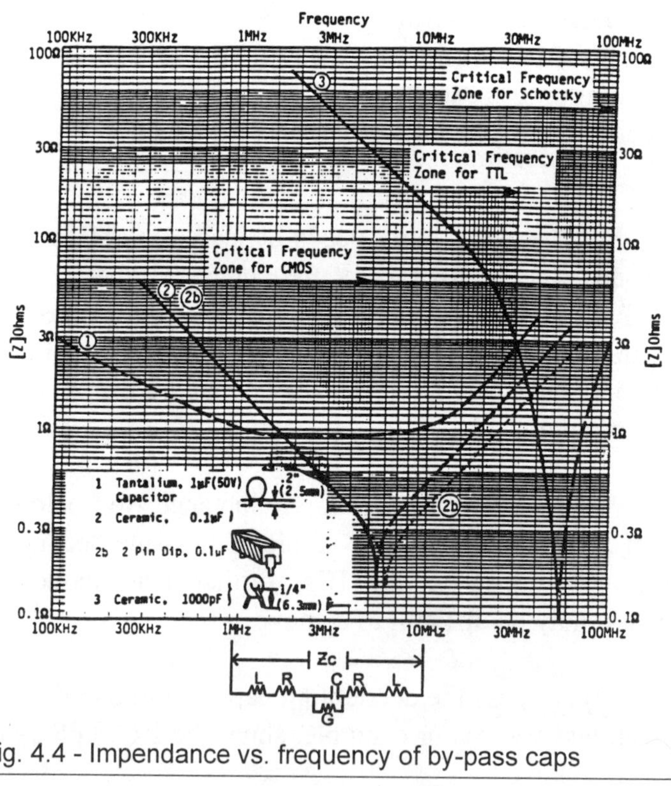


Fig. 4.4 - Impendance vs. frequency of by-pass caps

some typical PCB-discrete capacitors. It is clear that non-surface mount caps will not perform above 100 MHz for the examples shown.

## 4.5 Surface-Mount Caps and their Performance

Several manufacturers offer a variety of SMT caps as well as built-in caps to the ICs. A few are now discussed.

Figure 4.5 shows one manufacturer's catalog data on surface-mount, feed-thru capacitors. The data are difficult to interpret since the *installed* series inductance values are not included. Naturally, such parasitic inductance will reduce the resonant frequency. This could be estimated by adding specified values, such as 3, 5 or 10 nH. Then, calculations similar to those made in a previous section will produce better expectations of *insitu* performance.

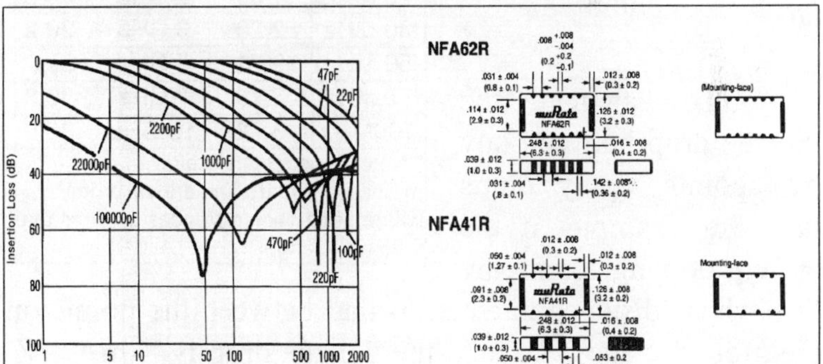


Fig. 4.5 - Surface-mount, feed-thru capacitors

Built-in SMI IC caps can result in equivalent series inductance of 1 to 2 nH. If the total chip decoupling cap is distributed to several locations on the chip, then each cap value is reduced as well. By combing both practices, the resulting LC product can be reduced 10-50 times. From Eq. (4.6), the self-resonant frequency increases $1/\sqrt{LC}$ or about five time to 150 MHz in the example.

## 4.6 Power Ground-Plane Impedance

The impedance of a one-ounce, copper-foil ground plane is listed in Tab. 4.1. The one-oz corresponds to a typical PCB foil thickness of 1.4 mils (36 microns). The impedance is given in milliohms/ square and corresponds entirely to inductive reactance.

**Table 4.1 - Impedances* of a One-Ounce Copper Ground Plane**

| Freq. | Imped. | Freq. | Imped. |
|---|---|---|---|
| 1 MHz | 1.01 | 100MHz | 3.72 |
| 2 MHz | 1.10 | 200MHz | 5.22 |
| 3 MHz | 1.17 | 300MHz | 6.39 |
| 5 MHz | 1.29 | 500MHz | 8.25 |
| 7 MHz | 1.39 | 700MHz | 9.76 |
| 10 MHz | 1.53 | 1 GHz | 11.6 |
| 20 MHz | 1.89 | 2 GHz | 16.5 |
| 30 MHz | 2.20 | 3 GHz | 20.2 |
| 50 MHz | 2.71 | 5 GHz | 26,0 |
| 70 MHz | 3.15 | 7 GHz | 30.8 |
| 100MHz | 3.72 | 10 GHz | 36.9 |

* Note: impedances are given in milliohms/ square and are valid only where separation distances are less than 0.05 wavelength.

To calculate the voltage drop between any two points, apply ohms law. For example, if the current flowing across any line whose distance is equal to that between the points on the ground plane is X mA, the voltage drop is X mA * Z. To illustrate, assume in a one cm length, 10 gate return currents = 200 mA at a clock frequency of 50 MHz. The voltage drop is 0.2 amps x 2.71 mohms = 0.54 millivolts. This clearly shows that voltage drops in a ground plane are insignificant relative to the noise-immunity levels of logic. However, if the packing density is intense, these levels can increase by one or two orders of magnitude to result in a significant ground bounce.

For power-ground plane power distribution, the impedance corresponds to the characteristic impedance of the power system. Tab. 2.3 in Chap. 2 gives the values for a wide-range of geometry. Typical values may range from 100 mohms to one ohm. So toggling gate currents of 20 mA may result in voltage drops of the order of 10 mV. Thus, even power-ground plane, power distribution does not result in insignificant voltage drops. This, again, is why decoupling caps are required at individual ICs to minimize local $V_{CC}$ supply sag.

The capacitance, C, of the power-ground plane distribution layers is:

$$C = 8.84\ A\varepsilon_r/h \quad \text{pF} \tag{4.8}$$

where, A = area of plane in $mm^2$
h = power-ground plane separation in mm
$\varepsilon_r$ = relative board dielectric constant (default = 4)

<u>*Example:*</u> Many multilayer PCBs have layer separations of 5-10 mils (approx. 0.2 mm). The local capacitance of these planes corresponds to about 8.84 x 100 x 4/0.2 or approximately 20 $nF/cm^2$ of plane area. Unfortunately, this does not provide sufficient decoupling for densely-packed PCBs. Also the inductance of vias and DIP pins or SMT traces limit the high-frequency usefulness, so that decoupling caps are still required. However, with PCMCIA cards using layer heights of 2 mils

(0.05 mm), the capacitance approaches 100 nF/cm$^2$. In time, the dielectric constant of a power-ground plane may approach 100 or more (e.g., certain titanates) so that few, if any, decoupling caps may be required (except those located on the ICs).

## 4.7 Combating Power Dropouts.

AC power provided by the electrical utilities have power dropouts resulting in missing fractions or complete cycles of 60 (or 50) Hz power. They occur due to switching action in the substation switch yard in balancing phase load and power factor, and sometimes during electrical storms.

Most switching-regulator power supplies use smoothing filters in their $V_{CC}$ outputs corresponding to holdup times of about 25 mseconds. This means that the DC power will drop by 10% within the holdup time when source A-C power is temporarily absent. To prevent loss of volatile memory during a dropout, computers should add larger caps to their SMPS. Alternatively, the backplane or motherboard should have a NiCad or lithium battery added to holdup the $V_{CC}$ supply voltage during dropouts up to a few cycles to prevent loss of memory.

## 4.8 References

Drewniak, J. L.; Hubing, T. H. and Van Doren, T. P., Investigation of Fundamental Mechanisms of Common-Mode Radiation from PCB with Attached Cables, *IEEE International Symposium on Electromagnetic Compatibility,* 1994, pp. 110-115.

Heinke, R., "EMC Controlled PCB Design," Conference Record of the EMC EXPO, *Interference Control Technologies, Inc.*, 1989.

Montrose, M. I., "Overview of Design Techniques for Printed Circuit Board Layout Used in High-Technology Products, *IEEE International Symposium on Electromagnetic Compatibility,* 1991.

Paul, C. R., "Effectiveness of Multiple Decou;ing Capacitors," *IEEE Transactions on Electromagnetic Compatibility,* EMC-34, pp. 130-133.

White, Donald R. J., "EMI Control in the Design of Printed Circuit Boards and Backplanes," *Don White Consultants, Inc.*, 1982.

# Chapter 5

# Analog, Clock Circuits and Data Lines

This chapter addresses the principal PCB radiators: clock circuits, clock distribution and IC interconnect data lines. Since radiation from traces is proportional to their magnetic moments (IA), their current and trace circuit-loop areas are to be minimized. This impacts crosstalk for similar reasons.

PCB radiation pickup from hostile ambients and ESDs share the loop area problem as well.

Where on-board analog circuits are involved, they must be isolated from digital return-circuit current flow. They typically have sensitivities three orders of magnitude greater than their logic mates.

## 5.1 The Analog Problem

Like acid and water, digital and analog circuits don't mix. Digital circuits, with noise-immunity levels in the order of 1 volt, are immune to analog current low and corresponding voltage drops. The reverse, however, where analog circuits can have mV sensitivities in an environment of a few volts digital swing, are troublesome.

The best approach is not to use digital and analog on the same PCB. Or, if they must share a PCB, isolate them (i.e., protect the analog) as much as possible. This suggests that they be located far apart on any PCB and to use opposite ends of an edge connector or use different connectors altogether. These and moats are discussed in Chap. 8.

But, what if an A/D or D/A converter is involved? Figure 5.1 shows an analog-to-digital converter on a*Analog, Clock and Data Lines* double-sided, single-layer board. They are sharing the same $V_{cc}$ power source and signal return traces - a dangerous practice. As shown in the equivalent circuit, a portion of the digital return-circuit current is flowing through part of an analog trace return. Thus, common-impedance noise coupling will limit the useful lower level to which the analog may be digitized.

The corrected circuit in Fig. 5.1 shows the digital and analog with their separate dedicated return traces to the edge connector. However, they must be connected at one point to ensure the digitizing process is digitizing the correct analog level and not some other range. Since it is a single-point connection, no digital current return can flow

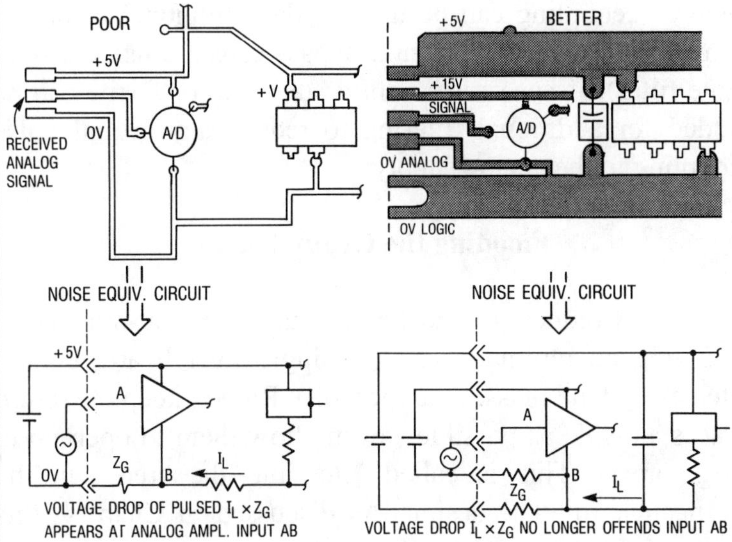


Fig. 5.1 - Avoiding common return noise in an A/D converter

through the analog traces. Also, ensure that the connection is made at the A/D circuit and not at a point well removed or off the PCB where path lengths of traces or wires can be different resulting in differential-mode coupling.

Sharing the common return path in Fig. 5.1 is only half of the EMI problem. Both digital and analog are fed from the same power source to result in common-impedance coupling through the same $V_{CC}$ supply trace. The best fix is to provide dedicated power supplies. This is achieved from different secondary taps on the SMPS output transformer. Alternatively, a D/C-to-D/C converter may be used.

In an effort to avoid a separate analog power supply, heavy decoupling can be used at the common $V_{CC}$ bus in which both SMT ferrites and bypass caps are used (a two-pole filter). If necessary, a third stage cap or ferrite can be added for additional filtering to reduce any digital noise coupling to the analog supply.

## Flooding the Ground Areas

To reduce ground bounce and common-impedance coupling on return traces in a single-layer board, do not etch away land masses (copper foil). Rather, keep the return traces as wide as possible - even allow them to open up to large areas. This is called "flooding the areas" in the vernacular of PCB design. As discussed in Chap. 4, this will reduce the ground return-path impedance from two to four orders of magnitude over that of an isolated ground-trace return. This is shown in Fig. 5.2 for the before and after situation. To prevent PCB warping, approximately the same amount of copper foil should be removed from both sides of the SLB.

Another approach to the above, discussed in Chap. 8, is to add a moat around the analog area, and to bridge the moat with filtered power and data lines.

**(A) Too Thin 0-Volt and +VCD Traces. Also, High Impedance Thin Copper Border Around PCB Card Will Act as a Pick-up Loop**

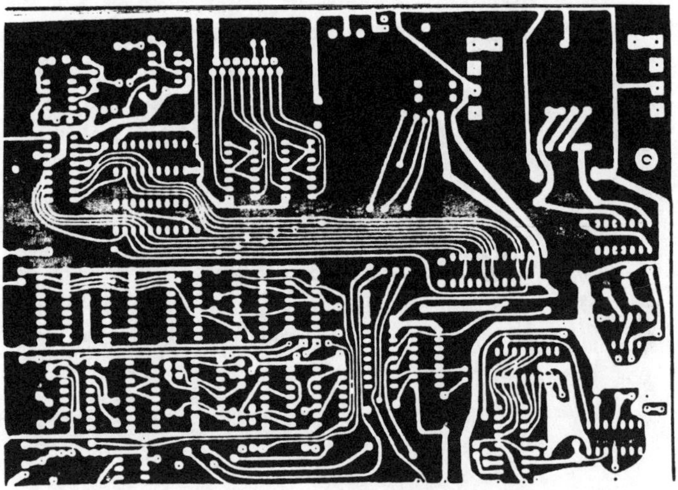

**(B) Ground & Power Traces have been Enlarged - Copper has been Left (Not Etched) Wherever Possible**

Fig. 5.2 - Flooding the ground areas for noise reduction

## 5.2 R-F Demodulation

From an EMI immunity point-of-view, another reason that analog or logic can *crash* is when radiation from a nearby walkie talkie, cellular phone or ESD reaches high enough levels. For this, coupling into trace ground loops can exceed the sensitivity of the analog or noise-immunity level of the logic family.

However, the above scenarios correspond to low-level transmitter carrier radiations (or risetimes for ESD) that exist outside the passband of the logic family. As discussed in the reference, audio rectification, sometime called R-F demodulation, can result in analog and digital device malfunctions. The base-emitter interface of the transistor acts like a second detector in a superheterodyne receiver, dumping the carrier and passing the modulation to result in a device crash. Fixes for this are basically the same as those discussed in Chap. 3 for reducing PCB radiation, since most failures involve coupling into and out of trace-loop areas. Filtering (filter-pin connectors, ferrites or bypass caps) at the I/O connectors also becomes a solution as discussed in Chap. 10.

## 5.3 Clock Circuits and Guard Traces

Clock circuits and their interconnect traces are often thought to be the biggest source of radiated EMI from PCBs. Actually, radiation from IC interconnect traces are usually significantly greater since there is many times more of them than clock traces. Nevertheless, clocks need special attention.

Here are a few practices to follow. Do not use all of them at any one time since an overkill may result:

- Locate clocks toward the center of PCBs and away from board edges and I/O areas and connectors.
- Do not use sockets since sockets add inductance and increase radiating path length and loop areas.
- Use a localized ground plane for clock circuits. Bond the clock plane to the main ground plane layer through several vias.
- Use component shields on clocks and clock drivers.
- Route clock distribution traces through internal PCB layers and terminate in resistor pads for impedance mismatch buffering.
- Hand route clock traces on the component side of board and use guard traces with frequent via grounds.

Figure. 5.3 shows a local ground plane used for clock circuits. Located on layer-1, the ground plane is connected to the signal-return ground plane through a number of vias. The purpose of the local ground plane is to reduce radiation, since from one of the boundary conditions to Maxwell's equations, the tangential electric field goes to zero at a metal conductor (ground plane) interface.

Where clock traces exit from the clock driver, one of two options exists:

(1) Go down to lower levels, preferably between two ground planes, and rout the traces therein. This reduces clock radiation from the PCB traces to nil levels.

(2) Protect the clock lines with guard traces on the outer layer-1. Pin these guard traces through vias to the ground plane at least every 0.02 wavelength (in the dielectric media) of the clock frequency. This corresponds to pinning about every 6 cm for a 50 MHz clock in a PCB layer having a relative dielectric constant of 4.

As it develops, guard traces are somewhat more effective in reducing crosstalk than radiation. Thus, option

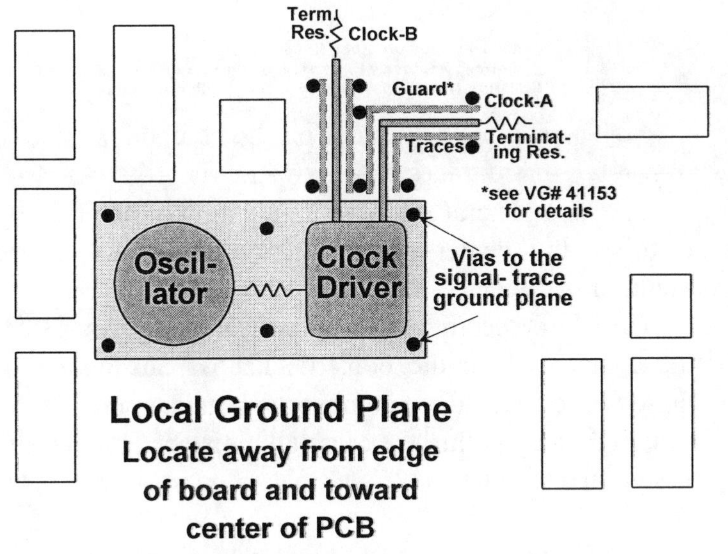


Fig.5.3 - Local ground plane for clock circuits

#(1) is more effective in reducing clock trace radiation from PCBs.

Figure. 5.4 shows how guard traces are routed for clock and sensitive data lines. More than one line may share guard traces for part of the path length. Options to this are:

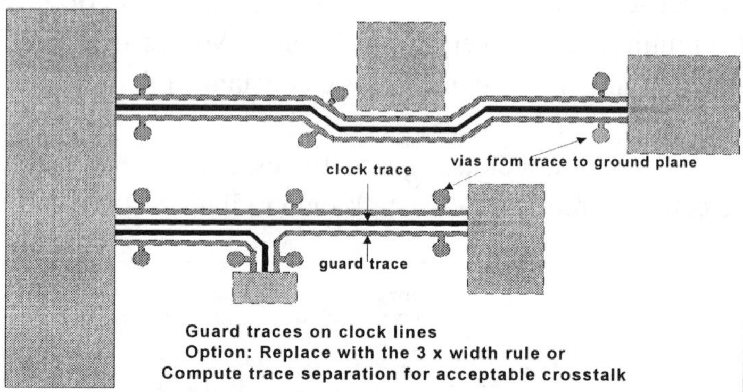


Fig. 5.4 - Clock and sensitive-line guard traces

(1) As a general rule, separate parallel trace run by three times the center-to-center trace width to reduce crosstalk, or

(2) More specifically, use software program #3850 in the floppy disk in the book pocket (if this option to purchase was exercised) to compute crosstalk. Separate by an amount to keep within the crosstalk noise budget. This is discussed further in Chap. 7.

## 5.4 Impedance Discontinuities and Control

For clock and data frequencies below roughly 30 MHz (actual criteria is explained later), where wavelength in many dielectric materials is about 5 meters, impedance discontinuities from driving gate to driven gate are unimportant. However, at higher frequencies, impedance mismatching can result in altering the voltage swing as seen at the driven gate. This, in turn, affects the wave shape and creates pulse backporching, wave distortion and in extreme cases, ringing. All this consumes the noise-immunity budget and leads to bit-error rates and other performance degradation.

There are three factors in PCB design that will now be discussed which impact impedance discontinuities: (1) source, line and load impedances, (2) vias and layer jumping and (3) trace configurations.

### 5.4.1 Source, Line and Load Impedances

The issue here involves transmission-line theory. Since this is well beyond the scope of this handbook, only some basics are discussed. The transmission line in question is the interconnect trace from an IC driving gate to another IC driven gate.

If the driving-gate impedance, microstrip or strip-

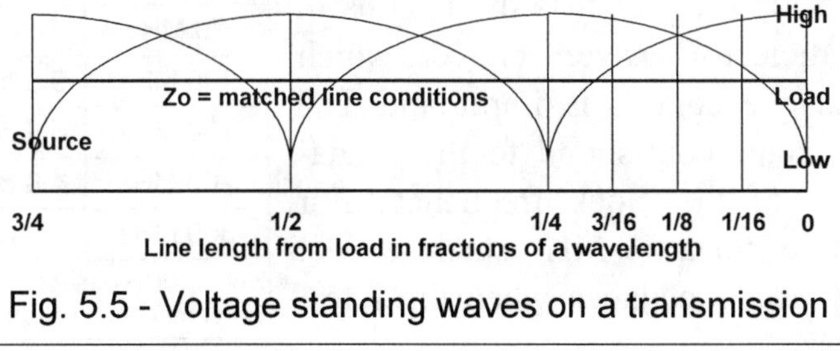


Fig. 5.5 - Voltage standing waves on a transmission line

line transmission line, and driven gate impedance were all approximately equal, no problem would result. But, this is not the case. For example, many gate source impedances are about 10-20 ohms, gate load impedances are 80-300 ohms, and line impedances are 30-60 ohms. These produce VSWRs (voltage standing-wave ratios) in long lines of roughly 3:1 at either or both source and load. This means that resulting voltage swings at the driven gate may vary from nearly $V_{CC}$ to less than half the intended swing - a clearly intolerable situation.

When the length, L, of this interconnect transmission line is short compared to a wavelength at the clock and data-line fundamental frequency, i.e., $L<\lambda/16$, then the impedance effect of the intervening line becomes negligible. This is illustrated in Fig. 5.5 showing the standing waves on a transmission line.

The approximate critical length ($L_m$ in meters and $L_{cm}$ in centimeters) in a PCB die- lectric material of $\varepsilon_r$, is:

$$L_m = \lambda_d/16 = \lambda_{air}/16\sqrt{\varepsilon_r} \qquad (5.1)$$

$$= 300/16f_{MHz}\sqrt{\varepsilon_r} = 19/f_{MHz}\sqrt{\varepsilon_r} \qquad (5.2)$$

$$L_{cm} = 950/f_{MHz} \qquad \text{for } \varepsilon_r = 4 \qquad (5.3)$$

Based on the $\lambda_d/16$ criterion and Eq. (5.3), Tab. 5.1 lists the lengths in the dielectric layer above which impedance control is important. The frequencies correspond to the fundamental of the clock frequency. For example, for a 50 MHz clock, expect to control impedance when the inter-

Tab. 5.1 - Critical length for impedance matching

| Frequency | Length |
|---|---|
| 10 MHz | 95 cm |
| 15 MHz | 64 cm |
| 20 MHz | 48 cm |
| 30 MHz | 32 cm |
| 50 MHz | 19 cm |
| 70 MHz | 14 cm |
| 100 MHz | 9.5 cm |
| 150 MHz | 6.4 cm |
| 200 MHz | 4.8 cm |
| 300 MHz | 3.2 cm |

Note: PCB dielectric constant of 4 is assumed

connect trace length exceeds 19 cm for a board dielectric constant of 4. Methods of impedance control are discussed later.

### *Risetime Propagation Criteria*

Another criteria for matching impedance or terminating the trace lines exists. This is based on the round-trip propagation time of the interconnect trace exceeding the risetime of the logic family.

The velocity of propagation, $V_p$, in the PCB dielectric material, $\varepsilon_r$, is:

$$V_p = 3 \times 10^8/\sqrt{\varepsilon_r} \quad \text{m/sec} \tag{5.4}$$

$$= 30/\sqrt{\varepsilon_r} \quad \text{cm/nsec} \tag{5.5}$$

The delay time, $t_d$, in transitioning a trace length is the reciprocal of Eq. (5.5):

$$t_d = \sqrt{\varepsilon_r}/30 \quad \text{nsec/cm} \tag{5.6}$$

The critical condition (avoiding ringing, back-porching, etc.) requires terminating the characteristic impedance of the interconnect traces of length $L_{cm}$ and exists when:

$$L_{cm} > \tau_r/2t_d = 15\tau_r/\sqrt{\varepsilon_r} \tag{5.7}$$

where, $\tau_r$ = risetime of the logic family

*Example:* if ACT logic family has a risetime of 3 nsec and the PCB has a relative dielectric constant of 4, the critical line length requiring termination of the interconnect transmission line from Eq. (5.7) is 22 cm. Normally, longer lengths of these amounts are obtained when one driving gate in a PCB is talking to another gate through the backplane.

### *Capacitive Loading*

Fanout (multiple gate loading in which a driving gate drives multiple driven gates) produces additional capacitance, $C_g$, to be added to the interconnecting microstrip or stripline. This impacts the propagation delay of Eqs. (5.6) and (5.7):

$$t_{dC} = t_d \sqrt{1+\frac{C_g}{C_o}} \qquad (5.8)$$

$$C_o = 1000\ t_d/Z_o \quad \text{pF/length} \qquad (5.9)$$

where, $C_g$ = Sum of each gate input capacitance
$C_{in}$ = 8-12 pF for TTL families
= 7-8 pF for CMOS families
= 3-5 pF for ECL families

*Example:* Using the same example of the ACT (CMOS) logic as above, determine the critical interconnected line length (assume $Z_o$ = 60 ohms) when eight ACT gates are driven from a single driving gate:

$$C_g = 8 \times 8\ \text{pF} = 64\ \text{pF}$$

$$C_o = 1000 \times 3/60 = 50\ \text{pF}$$

$$\sqrt{1+\frac{C_g}{C_o}} = \sqrt{1+64/50} = 1.51$$

From modified Eq. (5.7):

$$L_{cm} > t_{d.} = 15\tau_r/\sqrt{\varepsilon_r(1+C_g/C_o)} \qquad (5.10)$$

$$= 22\ \text{cm}/1.51 = 15\ \text{cm}$$

A later section in this chapter discusses termination techniques for PCB IC interconnects when the round-trip time propagation exceeds the logic family risetime.

### *5.4.2 Vias and Layer Jumping*

Vias are the only methods to get from one layer to another in PCB design and layout. They are an extension of the plated-through-the-hole concept. Vias may be developed as one or both of either types:

(1) Complete vias: from top to bottom layer in which any trace, requiring interconnection at different layers, does so at its via pad.

(2) Blind vias: internal to the multilayers in which only those interconnect traces needing connecting are so connected.

Vias offer many opportunities to control the layout routing for interconnecting traces. As mentioned in an earlier section, this is also important for controlling trace radiation, such as burying clock lines between ground planes.

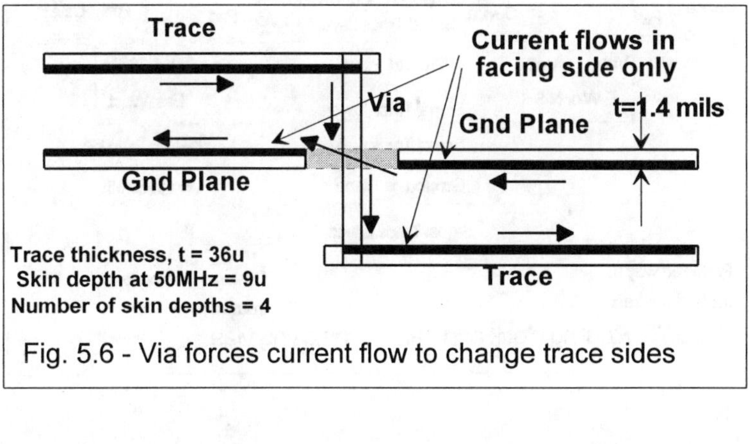


Fig. 5.6 - Via forces current flow to change trace sides

The self inductance introduced by a via in the trace path is roughly 2 nH. At 30 MHz, this corresponds to about 0.2 ohms and would seem to be insignificant compared to the characteristic impedance of the microstrip or stripline. However, vias disrupt the return-current flow in the ground plane as shown in Fig. 5.6. This results from the roughly 4 skin depths [one skin depth of 0.4 mils at 30 MHz for 1-ounce copper foil, 1.4 mils. See Eq. (2.3), Chap. 2]. Therein, return current flowing in the top skin of the plane has to readjust itself to flow in the bottom skin after transitioning a via.

This disrupted re turn-current path may correspond to an in- jected series imped- dance discontinuity of several ohms at 30 MHz.This begins to dis- turb the characteristic impedance of the ori- ginal interconnecting trace. So, it is apparent that the design objective is to minimize the number of vias or layer jumping for data lines exceeding 30 MHz to protect the noise-budget margin.

Figure. 5.7 illustrates some typical vias in the path of a clock or data line. Because of the impedance disruption

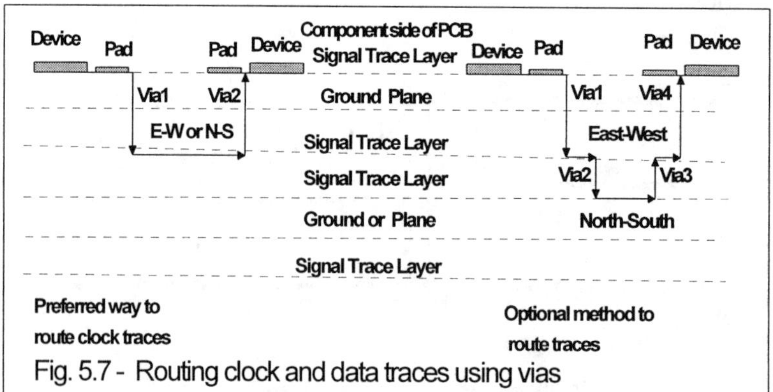


Fig. 5.7 - Routing clock and data traces using vias

to the interconnecting trace line, it is preferred to buffer the impedance mismatches at both source and load with resistance pads. This helps reduce the VSWR and pulse distortion and lower mismatch budget consumption.

### 5.4.3 Trace Configurations

High-speed data-line traces do not like to see abrupt changes in direction since this also causes an impedance mismatch resulting in pulse backporching, distortion and sometimes ringing. All this consumes some of the noise budget to make the PCB more susceptible to other EMI pickup.

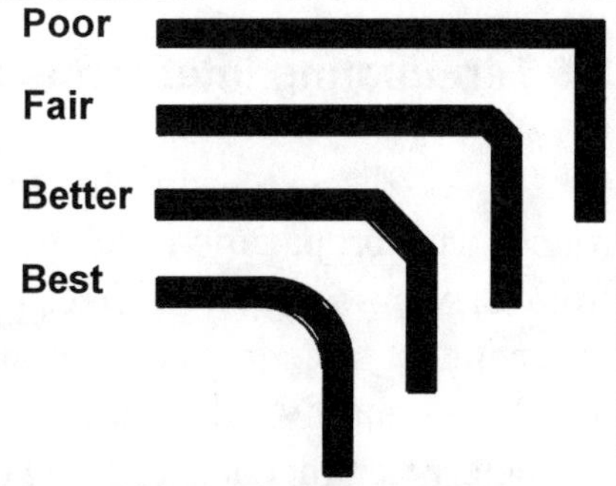


Fig. 5.8 - Directional transitions in trace configurations

Figure 5.8 shows four stages of trace direction changes ranging in performance from poor to best in impedance control. Current does not like to race around corners with- out undergoing some tendency to launch radiation or incur an impedance discontinuity. Think of it like race horses hugging the inside rail in going around corners at the race track. No one wants to go the longer route on the outside, where the impedance is greater.

In summary, interconnect trace impedance control from driving gate to driven gate is not important where frequencies are low or the trace length is short. For example, the longest dimension in a PCMCIA card is about

7 cm. So, impedance matching is unnecessary. However, when clocks and data lines begin to exceed about 100 MHz or their lengths exceed about 20 cm, things begin to get critical. With faster edge-rate logic coming into use, radiation and noise-budget conditions are likely to get worse except for small devices, such as PCMCIA cards.

## 5.5 Terminating Interconnect Traces

As discussed in the previous section, when the round trip propagation delay (elapsed propagation time from driving gate to its driven gate and return) in an IC interconnect trace transmission line exceeds the rise time of the logic family, the line must be terminated in its characteristic impedance, $Z_0$. This avoids pulse distortion due to backporching or ringing, which consumes the noise budget of the logic's noise-immunity level.

If more than one driven gate is involved, there are more than one input gate impedances in parallel which must be considered in impedance matching the gate loads to $Z_0$. This also assumes that the gates are close together so that their branch lines correspond to a small fraction, say 15%, of the interconnect line length to avoid impedance variations with length. Thus, do not daisy chain gates. Instead, use radial fanout traces to each gate from the center gate.

There are five methods which may be used to accomplish terminating interconnect traces. Sometimes, it may be necessary to use a combination of two to achieve the objective:

- Parallel termination
- Thevenin termination
- Series termination
- RC termination
- Diode termination

### 5.5.1 Parallel Termination

Figure 5.9 shows the generic form of parallel term-

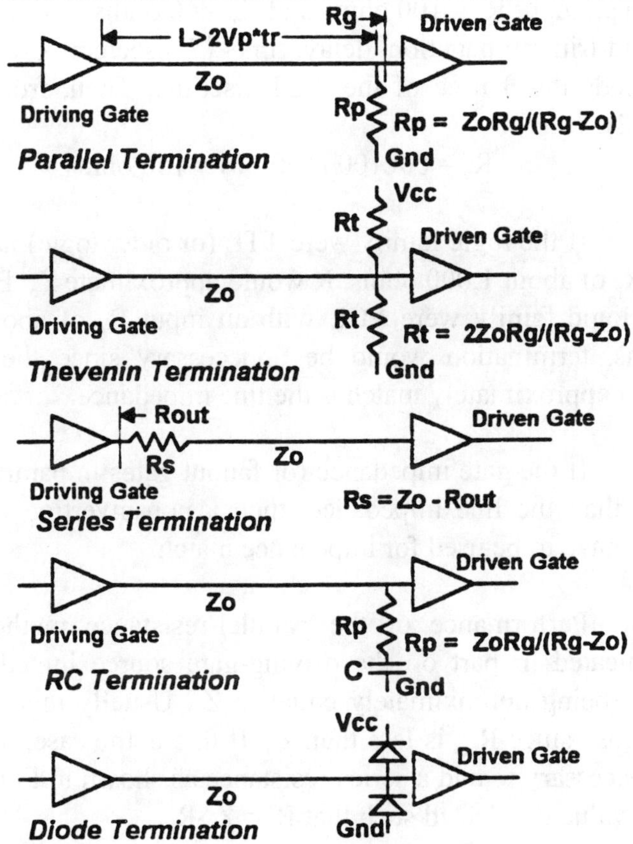


Fig. 5.9 - Typical impedance termination configurations

nation located at the input of the driven gate. Remember, that the input gate impedance (resistance = $R_g$) is in parallel with $R_p$. Thus, the parallel combination of $R_p$ and $R_g$ must approximate $Z_o$:

$$Z_o = R_pR_g(R_p+R_g) \quad (5.11)$$

or,

$$R_p = Z_oR_g/(R_g-Z_o) \quad (5.12)$$

*Example:* Assume that ACT logic is being used with an input $R_g$ = 100 ohms and $Z_o$ = 60 ohms, and that the round-trip propagation delay time (7 nsec/cm x length) exceeds the 3 nsec of the ACT risetime. Then, from Eq. (5.12):

$$R_p = 60*100/(100-60) = 150 \text{ ohms.}$$

If the logic family were TTL (or older logic) having an $R_g$ of about 1,000 ohms, R would approximate $Z_o$. But, if the logic family were ECL with an input $R_g$ of about 55 ohms, termination would be unnecessary since the gate input approximately matches the line impedance.

If the gate impedance (or fanout gates in parallel) is less than the line impedance, then a non-inverting buffer may have to be used for impedance match.

Performance of the parallel-resistance method is predicated in part on the driving-gate source impedance, $R_{out}$ , being approximately equal to $Z_o$. Usually this is not the case since $R_{out}$ is less than $Z_o$. If this is the case, it may be necessary to add a series resistance as shown in Fig. 5.9. The value is selected such that $R_s = Z_o$-$R_{out}$.

One of the disadvantages of parallel termination is that the parallel resistance, $R_p$, consumes $V_{cc}$ power.

### 5.5.2 Thevenin Termination

This method allows for achieving the correct termination for logic high and low conditions. It is calculated in a manner similar to that used in Eq. (5.9), except that $R_t$ = 2R or the parallel combination of the two resistors if not equal. This combination is best for TTL logic family.

### 5.5.3 Series Termination

Parallel or Thevenin termination matches the receiving end of the transmission line, but this may leave the sending end unmatched. To control the overall waveshape, the sending end must be terminated as well. This is achieved by adding a series resistance at the driving gate, such that its value plus that of the gate output impedance equals $Z_o$.

### 5.5.4 RC Termination

To overcome the wasted power in the parallel termination method, a capacitor, C, is added so that the $V_{cc}$ power is blocked except when switching. The value of the capacitive reactance of C should be less than about 10 % of $R_p$ at a frequency corresponding to the bandwidth of the logic family. For $R_p$ ranges of 50 to 300 ohms and logic risetimes of 1 to 5 nsec, C will approximate 1,000 pF.

Ensure that the series resonance of the installed C is at or above the logic family bandwidth ($1/\pi\tau_r$ - see Chap. 4) by using very-short cap leads, foil leads or SMT caps, as applicable.

### 5.5.5 Diode Termination

To reduce line ringing, a diode pair may be used to clip a negative overshoot on a mark one and a positive over-shoot on a space zero. However, the other techniques provide better performance since the interconnect transmission line should then not ring unless excessive vias are used.

## *5.6 References*

Dockey, R. W. and German, R. F., "New Techniques for Reducing Printed Circuit Board Common-Mode Radiation," *IEEE International EMC Symposium,* Dallas, Texas, August 9-13, 1993, pp. 334-339.

Heinke, R., "EMC Controlled PCB Design," Conference Record of the EMC EXPO, *Interference Control Technologies, Inc.,* 1989.

Mardiguian, M., "Controlling Radiated Emissions by Design," *Van Nostrand Reinhold,* 1992.

Montrose, M. I., "Overview of Design Techniques for Printed Circuit Board layout Used in High-Technology Products, " *IEEE International Symposium on Electromagnetic Compatibility,* 1991.

Motorola, "Semiconductor Mater Selection Guide," 09/95, Revision 8, Motorola, Inc.

White, Donald R. J., "EMI Control in the Design of Printed Circuit Boards and Backplanes," *Don White Consultants, Inc.,* 1982.

# Index

## A



## B

## C



## D

## E



## F

## G



## H



## I

## J-K-L



## M



## N-O

## P-Q



## R



## S

## T



## U-V

## W



## X-Y-Z